THE CHRIST SPARKS

Other books by William Bloom

Findhorn Press

Sacred Times — A New Approach to Festivals

First Steps — An Introduction to Spiritual Practice

Other publishers

Devas, Fairies and Angels

Meditation in a Changing World —
An Introduction to Individual and Group Meditation

The Sacred Magician

The New Age (editor)

The Seeker's Guide (edited with John Button)

Personal Identity, National Identity
and International Relations

THE CHRIST SPARKS

~~~~

THE INNER DYNAMICS OF GROUP CONSCIOUSNESS

William Bloom

FINDHORN
Press

British Library Cataloguing-in-Publication Data.
A catalogue record for this book is available
from the British Library.

Set in Palatino by Findhorn Press

Cover and author photographs by
Findhorn Foundation Visual Arts

Cover design by Posthouse Printing

Printed and bound by Guernsey Press Ltd,
Guernsey, Channel Isles

Published by
Findhorn Press

The Park, Findhorn,
Forres IV36 0TZ, Scotland
01309-690582 / fax 690036
e-mail thierry@findhorn.org

Contents

To all the children — those within you
and those within every aspect of
All That Is

The Christ Sparks

To my daughter, Sophia,
and all the
extraordinary souls of her generation

William

Foreword

In the Spring of 1987 my partner, Sabrina Dearborn, and I were holidaying in California. We spent one night at Meditation Mount in Ojai. Lying happily in bed, I suddenly felt uneasy. There was a very subtle yet strange pressure inside my head pushing, it seemed, against the top left side of my brain. This unusual sensation was prompting me to talk. I was not comfortable.

I told Sabrina what was happening. Without a question or a pause — she comes from a family line of psychics — she said that I should just talk and let whatever wanted to speak, speak.

Embarrassed, I began to talk. I whispered and spoke very quickly. I spoke fast because I could feel my sceptical mind wanting to block the process. Speaking rapidly, I could ignore my questioning scepticism. I spoke a stream of information which explained many facets of Sabrina's history and psychology, and told her many new things. Sabrina said then, and still says, that the information completely changed her life.

I was surprised and pleased; and embarrassed and suspicious.

I had always been suspicious of psychics and channels. My own spiritual background was in the western mystical tradition and I liked the clarity of daily discipline, of a focus on practical service and of carefully seeking esoteric wisdom. Psychics and channels, with crystals and violet cloaks, were a species foreign to me and I was happy to keep them at a distance. In fact, I suppose, I was a spiritual snob. Sabrina's own psychism was something I could handle because of its accuracy, and because of her ever-questioning integrity.

But suddenly there I was, channelling.

Well, at least it seemed as if the information had been useful.

Over the next weeks, I returned a few times to the strange sensation of channelling. I was intrigued because everytime I did it, my consciousness expanded, I acquired insights and it felt good. If I did not understand what was going on in me or in someone else, I would go silent and invite this strange sensation into my brain. The channelling would then begin. I always spoke aloud, in a whisper and very fast. I usually lit a candle and my body was hunched up, as if I were hiding my face. I needed absolute calm around me.

It soon became clear to me that this new consciousness wanted to write a book and I began to slip off into places where no one would disturb me and talk directly into a cassette recorder. The first session for this book was dictated, for example, parked off a very quiet road in Ireland. It was during this first session that the consciousness identified itself as a benevolent virus, as a swarm of consciousnesses, a swarm of sparks. They had first come to Earth in the 1960's in order to help us pass from a way of life which mainly experienced isolation, into a new awareness and experience of group consciousness. The phrase 'Christ Sparks' passed immediately through my awareness and that name has stuck. At home we just call them 'The Sparks.'

When the dictation of the whole book was completed on the 7th October, it was transcribed into a manuscript. I did not do anything with this manuscript, but put it away in a cupboard. Only one person, Cary Meehan, who later helped to edit it, read it. In fact, I more or less forgot about the manuscript, even though I still remained in relationship with the Sparks.

The interesting question is why I forgot about the manuscript for over seven years. Perhaps it was just a matter of waiting for the right time. I am not really sure. I do know that I remained embarrassed by the fact that I had channelled a book. One of my personal problems is that of trying to resolve and integrate that I am both intellectual and psychic, both mystical and active in the world. In contemporary western culture, it is not easy to be those things either privately and publicly. In some way I have been wary of fully admitting my psychism.

Another factor perhaps is my attitude to education. Although I am suspicious of channels, I have in fact been deeply influenced and educated by several books that were channelled or telepathically communicated. The Alice Bailey books, the Agni Yoga series, the Seth books by Jane Roberts and A Course in Miracles are all magnificent, inspiring and intelligent. I did not want, perhaps, to publish a channelled book that I was not confident was of a similar quality.

I also questioned from the very beginning, of course, whether I was accessing an aspect of my own psyche and that is a question which has remained with me ever since. After eight years of the experience, my own understanding is that I am not channelling a subtle part of my own consciousness and that I am genuinely channelling something beyond myself. When I read the manuscript I recognise passages that are very close to my own way of perception and communication, but this is perhaps inevitable and possibly one of the reasons why the Sparks chose to work through me. If the Sparks are just an aspect of myself, it is a fabulous way to write a book. I have written other books and know the hard work that goes into them. This one was a breeze. I just sat down and dictated. Session to session, I never gave the material a thought. This is every writer's dream — except that, wryly, you cannot own it as your own.

Anyway I 'forgot' about the manuscript . Seven years later, as I was clearing up my room and doing a periodic clear-out, the Sparks manuscript fell out of the cupboard. I greeted it with a smile and read a few pages. 'Hm', I grunted, it was not bad. In fact, I liked both the tone and the content. It seemed valuable. We had a friend staying with us and I asked whether she would look at a few pages and tell me what she thought of it. I went out of the house, came back later that afternoon and, to my surprise, found that Chris had not been able to put it down and wanted a copy for herself. The next day another friend, Allen, came round and I asked him also to look at it. Like Chris, he engaged with the manuscript immediately and said it should be published. 'Hm', I grunted again.

A few days later, very casually, I sent it up to my friends at Findhorn Press, asking whether they would take a peek at it. Thierry and Karin were also immediately grabbed by it and phoned me within a few days saying they wanted to publish it.

'Hm'.

So, here we are. I am the reluctant channel of this book you now hold in your hands. You will be glad, I hope, to know that my wariness has melted away and that I now feel warmly pleased that it is being published. This is partly because everybody involved has been so friendly and gently enthusiastic about it. It is a very nurturing process for me. The intellectual in me is melting; some anxiety has healed. This is all good for me.

Reading it again seven years after it first came through, I am struck by how much of the information in it is part of my normal understanding of life. My friends who have read it, all say about the information, 'Of course, I knew that. Its just that I didn't know it consciously.' I agree with nearly all of it myself, but there are a few places that I have reservations. Some parts I like a lot and I find myself saying very paradoxically, 'Mm, I wish I had written that.'

The Sparks present a new way of understanding

the interconnectedness of consciousness and life. Anyone who senses or is already aware of the changes that seem to be taking place in group awareness—at a personal and a planetary level—will find here an explanation that deepens our whole sense of holistic awareness. Many mystics have described every aspect of the world as being folded in within every particle of existence. Everything that is, is present in every particle that is. The Sparks say that they have come to help us fully experience that reality.

We live in a fantastic universe. Experience, consciousness and reality are unconditional and unlimited. For me, the Christ Sparks are part of that expansion into the infinite.

William

London, 1995

1

Introduction
~~~~
## The Avatar of Synthesis
and the
Christ Sparks

*This is the 10th August. Its half past three in the afternoon. I'm on the hard shoulder of the road out of Galway to Dublin. (Loud traffic noise in background.) This is going to be the first session with the Christ Sparks — if it comes through.*

*(Here we come!)*

We are extremely happy that we are at last able to begin writing this book through our mediator. We call ourselves the Christ Sparks because we find that phrase to be appropriate for the culture into which we are currently incarnating. We are Sparks because we are many units of consciousness, not simply one. We work as if we were a cloud or a swarm. If we were to communicate with an individual simply as one unit of consciousness then our point of focus would be so intense that it would hurt not only ourselves but also the individual with whom we were communicating. When we speak of our communicating with an individual we do not mean what is happening at the moment with William. We do not mean that communication is taking place at a telepathic level.

Our general method of communicating is to infiltrate the general vibration of the cellular make-up of the human personality. We infiltrate in this way so that individuals begin to experience themselves as something more than they actually are. The new experience in which they participate, which is triggered by us, is an experience similar to our experience of ourselves as units of consciousness. We are a swarm of Christ Sparks. We work together and have total rapport. We work as one form. As we incarnate into the psyches of individuals, they begin to experience themselves as life-forms which are intimately connected with all other life-forms on this planet and throughout the cosmos.

You will begin to understand then that the nature of our communications, and the nature of our purpose in being incarnate upon the planet, is to do with what is called Group Consciousness. We are going to use William to write a series of passages concerning the total nature of group consciousness. This is a subject which is crucial for all disciples working in the New Age, yet the subject is not properly understood. (By 'disciple' we mean any person whose major life purpose is spiritual change. In a way of course, this means everyone.) We want to share about this experience which is now available to humanity under the new dispensation of energies. In particular we wish to communicate about an energy that began incarnating into this planet approximately twenty-five years ago, though its intention to do this long preceded the action. This energy is known as the Avatar of Synthesis.

The Avatar of Synthesis is an extra-spatial consciousness belonging to realms beyond this galaxy. We do not here wish to stimulate any thoughts concerning unidentified flying objects or extra-terrestrial beings. What we are talking about are energy dimensions, modes of consciousness, which exist in the cosmos and which are naturally in resonance with everything else in the cosmos. It was only recently that it became appropriate for them to become a part of Earth's experience.

A human being walking her or his path may sound out a note to invoke and create a certain experience — that is to say she may be looking for a certain kind of happening to help her through her spiritual process. By this subconscious invocation, she can actually draw unto herself another person who will work with her to bring the experience she needs into reality. In the same way, the planet Earth and humanity as a whole can sound out a note which evokes from another part of the Cosmos an energy being and a consciousness. This cosmic energy being and consciousness *responds* to the need of the planet and of humanity. The Avatar of Synthesis is just such a cosmic energy being. It incarnated specifically through certain physical human communities some twenty-five years ago. Two of those well-known communities are Findhorn and Auroville.

At the same time that this particular Avatar incarnated, we incarnated alongside it. We are not part of the Avatar of Synthesis. We are units of consciousness who have experience which enables us to work cooperatively with it.

Since we first came into contact with William he has questioned us about the nature of our source. We are Units of Consciousness similar to human souls, except that the human soul is a far more rounded and experienced consciousness than we are. We do not have the depth of history that human souls have, but we do have a certain experience which allows us to understand in every given second the gestalt — the network and the framework — of impulses that creates the reality which is now, which creates the reality which is the moment.

We are by our very nature *electric*, electric sparks

of consciousness. We exist as tingles of consciousness, dancing sparks of consciousness. We have our own experience and own history, but our work now, for our own evolution, is with other forms of consciousness who are not electric sparks and who are held by time and space.

Human consciousness, by its very nature, has to proceed through time and space as if in a tunnel. We do not experience that tunnel. We experience ourselves as sparks in eternity. Like devic-angelic life-forms we simultaneously know the beginning and the end. We know this in a transcendent dimension which is separate from the tunnel that is your form of life-processing in time and space.

As we incarnate into Planet Earth we have a clear sense of the patterns of potential for cooperation which exist between human life-forms. We understand and perceive here and now that all consciousness on this planet is intimately interlinked. Now this is a philosophy, that all consciousness is interlinked, which at the moment is only an intellectual notion for most thinkers of humankind. In the New Age movement, in the metaphysical movement, it is only an *ideology* — that human beings are perpetually interrelated in consciousness and that everything is interlinked. We use the word 'ideology' carefully, because by it we mean simply a set of ideas which guide action — but not an experience. *Our* experience of the interdependence of consciousness upon this planet is not an experience of a set of ideas. It is an experience which exists in the moment here and now — and we are frustrated, so to speak (but not in reality), by the fact that even the most sophisticated human disciples are having problems surrendering to the actual experience of interdependence.

*B*efore we progress with an historical survey of how it is that human consciousness is now ready for this leap forward into a state of consciousness which we experience perpetually and easily, we wish to make just a few statements about the nature of our relationship with William. We would like to express for his sake, and for the reader's sake, that he is approaching this dictation-work with a caution which is fully understandable. He has said to us already that unless we come up with information that is more sophisticated than that which he himself produces, and which is at least as insightful, then he wants nothing to do with us. And we respect this totally.

We also accept the fact that in the planetary culture at the moment it is becoming something of a vulgarity to be a channel for entities which are not a part of one's own consciousness. We would like to state, however, very clearly that we are not in any way a part of William's own consciousness. We are not a part or an aspect of William's own inner or higher self. We are not in any way a part of his multidimensionality. We are beings in our own right — units of consciousness in our own right — and we are grateful for this opportunity to communicate.

*End of Introduction.*

# 2

# Why
# Human Separativeness?

We wish in this section to discuss the history of human consciousness as seen specifically from a level of inner dimensionality, which is that of the soul.

Let us be clear that it is indeed true that all psyches emerged out of the one psyche. At an electro-magnetic level of consciousness that is more dynamic, more fluid, than the level of consciousness that is experienced day by day, all consciousness experiences itself as unity. However, as is obvious from the daily experience of human incarnation, this sense of unity is not the nature of every-day consciousness.

In everyday consciousness humans do not experience themselves as being part of one interconnected network throbbing with the life of mystical divinity. Nor do they experience themselves as cells that are organically connected in one wonderful cosmic creature. It is certainly true that women and men are happy to adopt these ideas of interconnectedness as something that is intellectually acceptable and which resonates with a certain mystical sense of romance that they have. However the real experience of interconnectedness is one that only comes with heightened moments of ecstasy and mystical bliss. Even then those heightened moments are experienced in a form of transcendent consciousness from which human beings become separated the moment they return to their every-day consciousness.

The memory of that mystical experience is not one of interconnectedness, not one that demonstrates to them in the very fabric of their psyches that they are one with *everyone* else. The memory is of an experience that demonstrates their connectedness with the source of *spirit* and the source of *divinity*. Mystical experiences and ecstatic bliss lead individuals onwards in their relationship with Spirit. They instinctively attempt to move faster down the tunnel of time to completion in pure spirit.

But what we are describing here is the beginning of a new process in which mystical experience and ecstatic bliss include more than the experience simply of a high transcendent consciousness with which the human being aspires permanently to connect — as if building a path upwards and inwards and requiring great striving to achieve. What we are describing here is a new form of mystical experience which is more than the interconnectedness with the divine, which now includes interconnectedness with all life upon the planet, including *all human life*.

Many human psyches have this interconnected experience with nature. Throughout history, women and men have contemplated with nature and experienced their true fellow-creaturehood with nature and sometimes with their close biological or natural families. Despite the apparent savageness of nature in some of its forms, most humans can be caught by the cellular resonance of the mutual creaturehood they share with all natural life upon the planet. Depending upon the type and make-up of the individual human psyche, the harmonious sense-of-unity will be with minerals — or landscape — or plants — or animal life. People can feel, sense and experience unity with Nature. But there then exists a gap.

The gap is between the experience of oneness with, at one end of the scale natural life and the experience, at the other end of the scale, with divine life. In between there is the realm of humanity with which people do not experience oneness. What we are describing here is a new experience — of oneness with human life — of the possibility and reality of ecstatic wholeness with humanity.

We want to describe it not as an ideology, but as an experience which throbs through every cell of the human psyche. Humanity is one, and each of us is one with it. We wish to focus now on exactly why it is that individual humans — no matter how powerful and pure their devotion, no matter how powerful and pure their aspiration towards a sense of unity — nevertheless have difficulty experiencing this unity with their fellow human beings.

Let us be clear that the major pattern which has to be transcended here is one of *fear*.

It is not the experience of most human beings that their fellow creatures are to be trusted. It is not the ongoing minute by minute experience of most human beings that they can surrender themselves in trust to their fellow creatures.

~~~~

Session Two. Tuesday 11th August 6.30pm at the Grianan of Aileach

I feel a bit nervous about starting the session as I am still not perfectly certain that what is happening is not an aspect of my own consciousness. I was aware or I thought yesterday, that the Christ Sparks had not said enough about the exact nature of their consciousness and where they come from. They communicated with me between this session and the last and they explained that their consciousness had evolved along a path which I could understand as being similar to the group soul of a nest of ants, swarm of bees or flock of birds. Their particular mode of evolution had meant that they had retained their unity within a group soul yet had become self-conscious in the same way that humans are self-conscious. Thus they had achieved self-consciousness at the same time as being part of a group. They had achieved self-awareness while still remaining aware of their intimate connections as manifestations of the same group soul.

When I questioned them on where they actually came from, they said I knew absolutely nothing about astronomy and therefore there were no brain cell patterns of information on which they could usefully work to tell me where to go — other than to say, for example, "you go past Sirius and then take a sharp right." Ho, ho, ho!

All right, I'll begin the session now.

We wish to continue our discussion about the nature of man's sense of *separation* — correction, human beings' sense of separation — from their fellow humans, in opposition to the sense of oneness and unity they can achieve both with the other realms upon this planet and with transcendent realms of divinity.

Let us be clear that the cellular make-up of the human personality, psyche and physical frame is made up of cells which belong, and have belonged, to the realms of mineral, plant and animal. Locked into the memory patterns of the human body itself are patterns of memory to do with existence in those three previous realms. There is a realm consciousness of the different kingdoms locked into the human body. The human being, if she so wishes, can tap in at will to the memory functions of those particular realms. A woman, for example, can, if she wishes,

tap through the cells of her own body into the consciousness of the mineral kingdom and find there, through rapport, knowledge which was previously unattainable. This
sense of unity with the mineral kingdom, through attunement to its resonance in one's own body, is just the beginning of an intimate form of awareness, an educational discovery which has not yet been experienced even to one
per cent of its potential. This resonance can also be
achieved with the plant and animal realm.

The human cellular make-up does *not*, however,
hold such an attunement or sense of harmony in relation
to its fellow humans. Why is this?

The human psyche came about as a marriage between
the highest form of animal being and an incoming
extra-spatial form of consciousness. A spark of energy
was fired between certain evolved animal psyches and
certain extra-spatial consciousnesses. We can envisage
these extra-spatial consciousnesses as *angelic jewels*
brought into being, at a great point of tension, by distinct
cosmic psyches who work to manipulate energy at an
intersystemic level. The animals who were brought into
human consciousness were made to congregate at specific areas upon the surface of the planet where natural
vortices of energy exist. These vortices made it possible
to bring not just the animals' psyches, but also the actual
cell structure of their brains, up to a vibrational peak of
such intensity as to allow a form of electric contact to be
made with the extra-spatial consciousnesses — the
angelic jewels — who were incarnating into the planet.
The animals and extra-spatial consciousnesses merged.

Those extra-spatial jewels of consciousness are in a
sense devic-angelic, as they hold within themselves the
whole pattern, or plan, of both their history and their
unfoldment. When incarnate in form, they lose their sense
of transcendence and timelessness. But within their own

psychic field these jewels are simultaneously aware of all potentialities, past, present and future, knowing in the now their own completion. They have angelic awareness. We are, of course, describing human souls in their own dimension.

They themselves — the extra-spatial psyches — the human 'souls', entered into planetary life as part of a massive wave which responded to the needs of this planet for a dramatic move forward in its own evolution.

It is theoretically possible that the animal beings who represented the height of consciousness at that time could themselves have slowly evolved into a form of consciousness which could be recognised as distinctly human. However, the nature of this planet, and its history, were such that its progress was not fast enough for the whole of the planetary chain of which it is a part. Earth's progress is not only crucial from humanity's point of view, but also from the perspective of all the other planets with which it is associated, and from the perspective of the Solar Logos of which it is a part. Through the Solar Logos in turn, the planet's progress is important in relation to the other Solar Logoi with whom it forms a System.

As we say, it is possible that the highest forms of animal consciousness at that time could have been left alone to move forward slowly of their own accord. Their slowness, however, affected and held back all realms on the planet. This relative slowness of the evolution of the life-forms upon Earth, of the total psyche of Earth, was such that a note was sounded. This note was similar to the travail of a woman going through the pangs and physical pains of birth. It was a note of travail. The effort to bring those animal psyches forward into a heightened form of awareness was taking a terrible amount of effort. This was so great that it was creating psychic strain through all the realms upon the planet. One can talk about a point in Earth's history when the very mineral realm itself, the plant realm, and the whole of the animal realm, were struggling with the effort of pushing forward the psyches of the highest forms of the animal realm.

The effort was such that the whole planet was in pain. The psyche of the planet, therefore, sounded out this note of travail. And there is Divine Justice within the cosmos. All That Is has created within its extraordinary, playful imagination a system in which there is response to any need, rebound to any action.

This response came in the form of the jewels of consciousness — the souls — who were brought in to hover over and to be electrically incarnate in these animals.

Over a period of a few years, extra-spatial consciousnesses were brought into Earth's aura and anchored into the aura of these highly evolved animals. Self-reflection — the major attribute of humaneness — came about through the application of intense forms of cosmic prana and energy, bridging the animal realm, by an act of will from an outside hierarchy, into the realm of human consciousness.

(And just as a side note here we would note that if you go to geographical places of intense vortical energy you may find there, alongside the power if you care to meditate and attune to it, a resonance of the jewel form of consciousness, of the soul. If you are sensitive and resonant, you will find a note of the soul in its fulfilment. This is particularly so at a place like Glastonbury where one of the hills is especially associated with the note of the fulfilled soul.)

The reader should by now be becoming aware of the fact that the circumstances that existed upon this planet, which necessitated an external involvement in the evolution of its psyches, were not harmonious. This is indeed the case. We are talking here about something that is part of the cosmic history of planet Earth and of the cosmic history of the Logoic system of which Earth is a part.

The reason for the travail lies in this extremely ancient history when various cosmic psyches experimented with the solar system that existed before the solar system in which we exist now. This experimentation was unsuccessful and left behind energy-matter which had attempted to evolve — to jump forward into the solar system's intended future resonance — at too fast a rate. Energy-matter-consciousness was left behind which was dissonant with the fulfilment of the rest of the solar system. It had of course, to be healed and brought into the new and appropriate resonance.

Crucially, this energy-matter-consciousness *now* makes up the physical-etheric, emotional and mental stuff of planet Earth. And most crucially, from your perspective and experience, this energy-matter-consciousness from the previous system *makes up the cellular matter of the human personality*. This matter is healed, saved, re-resonated by the incarnating soul. As far as we are aware, this particular situation is unique to planet Earth and not similarly present in any other parts of the known cosmos. That is why Earth is developing a unique form of consciousness. It is the field where the mistake of a previous system is being rectified.

This is why there is interest from extra-spatial consciousnesses in Earth. The interest is not simply because of the need of Earth, similar to any other part of the system, to evolve — but because Earth demonstrates a highly unusual form of consciousness. Because of the unusual history of this energy- matter-consciousness on Earth and because of the ensuing difficulties inherent in bringing it back into an appropriate resonance, certain distinct notes or forms of awareness are brought about in the Earth's system, and in humanity in particular. These are usually only available to much more sophisticated psyches. The particular note that we are talking about here is that of *compassion*. It is a result of the healing role of your souls.

Compassion is an attitude and an energy which, at

the human level, is virtually unique to planet Earth and does not exist elsewhere in the cosmos at that level of consciousness. In the rest of the cosmos, what you on Earth know as compassion is an awareness and a state of being reserved purely for psyches that are of a Logoic nature. We ourselves were not fully aware or understanding of the nature of compassion until we came into incarnation here two decades ago. We have learnt about it over the last twenty years and it has been a very important part of our own growth processes. We now consider ourselves honoured and sanctified to have been able to integrate compassion into our own consciousness and experience.

The cells that make up the vehicles of the mineral and animal and plant kingdoms, though unique and extraordinary, exist in a form of harmonious happiness with each other. There is indeed a form of integrated symbiosis between the different realms upon the planet and no problems, as such, exist between them. There is a natural chain and cycle between them, a natural form of cooperation, a natural form of rhythmic dancing existence, which reflects the basic principles of the cosmos as a whole. This form of harmonious co-existence was, however, shattered at the time that the highest forms of the animal realm were brought into the form of consciousness which is self-reflective and human. The incoming note that was carried by the jewel consciousnesses, by the human souls, was such that it excited the animal brain cells in a way that they had never previously experienced.

The impact of self-reflectiveness upon the animal/human brain was such as to cause a form of electric irritation. The immediate result was not harmonious. With the beginnings of self-awareness and self-reflectiveness, there did not come any reflection upon the wonder and beauty of being alive. The nature of the awareness was such as to be psychically disturbing and irritating. The new humans, as they became self-aware of the natural rhythms and interdependence of life upon the planet, became confused, disorientated and frightened. Whereas previously there had been, in the cycles of life and death, an interpenetration of the different realms — an acceptance of the natural symbiosis of the system — self-reflection brought with it an awareness of *self-otherness*. This was unavoidable, yet brought with it more difficulties than had been expected.

The friction created in the brain cells by the introduction of the new awareness was such as to produce a form of natural dissonance and fear. The images of early humans, frightened in the forests and jungles, hiding in the trees, seeking safety in caves and in heights, are correct, poignant and deeply touching visions. It was indeed at this time that fire was introduced as a gift to the early human beings in order that the light and heat should bring them some comfort in an environment which they now found hostile.

As animal consciousnesses they had not found the environment hostile, but now developed into self-aware and self-reflective psyches, aware of their own finiteness, aware of their own terminability, aware of their own lack of safety — a dimension of self-conscious vulnerability now entered into their lives.

This vulnerability was experienced in relation to all the other realms upon the planet as well. The earth itself was unsafe in all sorts of ways — earth tremors, openings in the ground, volcanoes and so on. The plants themselves were also threatening in that many of them were deadly.

Previously there had been a natural rhythmic dance between animal-humans and plants, in that animal-humans knew instinctively which plants to eat. Now there were the beginnings of an inability to judge what was appropriate to eat and poisonings happened. As regards the animal realm, there were obvious physical threats.

Previously, you should remember, there had been an interpenetrating, symbiotic dance between all the kingdoms which had been accepted as appropriate. Now, however, in the human beings' new self-reflectiveness, there was an understandable fear.

But at a very basic level, there still existed in the cellular make-up of the human vehicles the memories of the symbiotic, comfortable, appropriate, harmonic relationship with the other realms. In the cellular make-up of the human bodies was the locked-in memory of the divine dance with these other realms, which was beautiful and comforting in its ecological wholeness and appropriateness. *There was not, however, any such memory of a similar type of relationship with their fellow human beings.*

The reader can see, therefore, that from the very beginning, locked into the human experience, there was a lack of memory of any form or cooperativeness with fellow human beings — because this cooperativeness had not previously existed. At the same time, as the new consciousness came into being, there was a sudden awakening to vulnerability.

Human beings were vulnerable not only to the realms of mineral, plant and animal, but also to each other. This sense of vulnerability came about from the natural ecological competition that existed to survive in any given geographical space. Subsistence was limited to certain numbers in a hunter-gatherer society because any given area could only sustain a certain quantity of humans. Equally, in other parts of the animal and plant realms, there was competition concerning mating. Moreover these factors of competition, in terms of local ecological support and mating, were exacerbated by the prolonged vulnerability of the human infant. We have, therefore, a picture here of early humanity existing in a state that held a high degree of primitive anxiety concerning each other. The notion of the noble savage living in harmony with his/her fellow beings is a mythical fiction. It is in the very essence of human history that there are difficulties in co-operating and that anxiety is experienced in human relations. Whereas there is a subconscious cellular memory of cooperation and symbiosis with the mineral, plant and animal realms — there is no such cellular memory of co-operation with fellow humans.

Now, we do not wish to say more at this moment concerning the history of humanity's evolution. We wish, however, to jump forward into the very moments of the present. We wish to say that just as those many millions of years ago when the highest realms of animal being were brought into self-consciousness as a result of the note of travail of the planet — so equally right now, we are in a time when there is an extra-spatial response to the travail of the psyche of the planet. We have mentioned already that the Avatar of Synthesis and we ourselves, the Christ Sparks, are forms of extra-spatial consciousness who have responded to the invocative call of the psyche of the planet. The nature of the Christ Sparks and the Avatar of Synthesis is to heal the sense of separation which exists between human beings.

We have described at the beginning of this section the nature of our consciousness and how our very evolution is based in the fact that we are one as in a group soul. We bring with us into the human psyche — as we incarnate in human beings — a healing and a new sense of wondrous adventure, of cooperation and of loving synthesis with all human beings upon the planet. We would like to underline the fact that this in no way demands the loss of individuality or any loss of the wonderful, eccentric forms of human personality that currently exist. We are talking about a new form of calm, a new form of ease. Just as in your vehicles there is a cellular memory of the cooperation with mineral, animal and plant realms, so too we are bringing with us a singing out into the cells of human beings the experience of loving cooperation with fellow humans.

3

Couples as Communities

This is Session Three, 12th August. Its 4.30 and I am at the Meitheal Community in Ireland. I am amazed at how fast these sessions are coming though and I have no confidence at all that anything fruitful will come through in this session. But, as usual, I will just roll along with the process. Okay.

Section Three: Couples as Communities.

In this section we want to move as fast as possible into discussing certain aspects which will be of immediate practical help to the readers of this material. We shall return later in our writing to more philosophical information about the nature of our being and the effect we are having at a macrocosmic level on the planet.

We wish to address particularly the nature of the problems that are now inherent in any two human beings coming together to form a romantic relationship or a relationship with a view to parenting. Marriage, as people in the metaphysical movement may have noticed, has been fast changing the rules and dimensions by which it is operated. In fact, it is frequently stated by people in the metaphysical movement that they do not know the rules for marriage and relationships.

The one rule, if any, that is now being brought in to

apply to serious relationships is that they are worth continuing just as long as there seems to be an inherent dynamic of psychological and spiritual growth in it for the two people involved. As soon as this no longer seems to be moving at a sufficiently rhythmic momentum, it is time to disengage from the relationship. This is so and appropriate. But what is required is some clarification about why it is that relationships have moved into this apparently new dynamic and some clarification about the difference between relationships now and in the past.

We would like to say first of all that we do not wish to ignore for one second the crucial matter of the joint responsibility that is incurred when a couple choose to breed together. We would look for a time — and some thinkers are already expressing this in your society — when there will be separate contracts for parenting. We do not want any situation in the future where such a thing as single parents exists, when a parent brings up children solely on the back of her or his own energy alone. We look forward to a time when, at the very basic level of understanding between a couple, it is recognised that there is a true community of responsibility for the children. This should not in any way be avoided by the apparent separation of the two people who came together in the marriage in the first place.

All that however, is a separate issue and that which we wish to discuss now concerns the dynamic psychological nature of the interrelationship between a man and a woman that can exist nowadays. We shall hold with the archetype of a man and a woman though we accept fully that there are many situations in which gay and lesbian relationship also hold within themselves the same form of power for growth and change. The major archetype, which must surely be recognised upon the planet however, is one of male and female — and as gay and lesbian relationships surely recognise, even within those forms of sexual relationship there also emerge archetypal patterns of male and female.

We are concerned here to discuss the nature of just how exactly it is that in the coming together of a man and a woman, what was previously just a simple form of marriage for procreation, has now developed into what appears to be a psychic duel of spontaneous combustion.

We should recognise that in the past couples came together for procreation and of course to satisfy sexual needs. Furthermore within most historical social systems and historical cultures it was considered appropriate to acknowledge the coming together of a couple for procreation by a rite of passage which introduced the couple to the mores of the social system within which they were to live. This ensured several things, not the least of which was the stability of the society in which the relationship took place and also the continuity of parenting. It should, however, be acknowledged that in some societies either the mother or the father have not been responsible for the rearing of the child — but other individuals, such as brothers, sisters, aunts, uncles and grandparents have been held responsible.

Over the last two thousand years, both the energy structure of the psychic dimensions of the planet and also the philosophies put forward by the various churches brought into marriage an aspect of sacred ritual. This is not to say that sacred ritual had not been an aspect of marriage before, but over the last two thousand years it was brought in in such a way as to engender an extremely powerful thought-form which says that marriage is two things: first, marriage is a form of sacrament and, second, marriage is a form of commitment.

The sacramental aspect for marriage and coupling was expressed in terms of the symbolic similarity between the joining together sexually of a man and a woman, and the joining together of a human personality and her/his own Spirit. The power for the experience of deep affection and love, and of the heightened electric awareness of orgasm, was deemed similar to the mystic's experience of bliss. As such, the churches wished to appropriate the relationship and, in a sense, to control what was a natural form of poetic creaturehood ecstasy and to turn it into a functioning aspect of a religious power hierarchy. The church also sought to impose upon marriage a form of commitment that resonated with Piscean ideals of devotion. In many ways you can perceive from these two interlinking patterns — first, that of society seeking stability and, second, that of the church seeking power — that marriage and coupling, far from being simply a playful union of sexual joy between two human beings following their natural instincts of creaturehood, became appropriated by the power systems of religious structure. Let us also draw into the argument here the understanding, presented in the previous section, concerning the innate fear and anxiety that human beings hold one for each other.

You can see here that we have a mixture of certain elements bound to act in a way that is dissonant and frictious with a naturally harmonious flow of affection and playful relationship. You may note then, that the nightmare which we are just describing, which is the essence of relationship — that is (a) the appropriation of the bliss of sex into becoming a sacrament of religion and (b) the necessity for a stable society, in Piscean patterns, projected into relationships as a form of stern commitment, and (c) the essential cautiousness, anxiety and hostility which humans have for each other — all these make an unpleasant brew that has interfered with what should be a natural mode of relationship.

Given simply that marriage over the last thousand years has been dramatically coloured by those three unpleasant elements, one can see clearly that human beings chose to begin to liberate themselves from those unpleasant and heavy patterns. A form of social revolution was bound to occur. That is happening now. It is only natural that human spirit expressing itself through personality should strive to achieve a form of relationship which is naturally more open and loving. It was also expected, as people noted, that as the planetary psyche moved out of the two thousand year cycle of Piscean energies into the Aquarian one, there would have to be new forms of relationship emerging.

We would like to stress, however, that the major crisis in relationships at the moment, and the major changes taking place in the basic nature of the structure for coupling is not due to the changeover from Piscean to Aquarian energies, though this indeed is contributory. It is not due either to the approaching resonance of the pure Christ energies, though this indeed is also relevant because it draws forth from humanity a desire for a more natural and affectionate way of relating to each other. We would claim that the dramatic change in their essential structure is due to the incarnation twenty years ago of the Avatar of Synthesis and of the accompanying consciousnesses, the Christ Sparks. It is we, therefore, who are taking responsibility for the friction and the pressure currently placed upon all of you.

You may smile wryly at our bare-faced cheek in this matter, but we reassure you that we are fully aware of the pain and anguish that it is currently causing. We are sympathetic and empathise with the poignancy of the current difficulties that exist, but we would like you to fully understand that our picture of *how it can be for you* is so beautiful that we have no qualms about the difficulties and changes taking place. We have a clear vision of the beautiful way of relating to each other that is possible for you and which is emerging for some of you already and which will be an experiential reality for most within your culture within the next fifty years.

Change is necessary to bridge into this new reality. And change by its very nature is painful. It is painful because the way in which you identify how you should be in relationship is shattered. You have been brought up as children and teenagers, and as young men and women, with certain images of the way in which you should behave in relationships and certain images of the commitment you should give. You now find yourselves in maturity acting in ways that are in variance with inner pictures that you have of yourselves. Be comforted by the fact that these pictures come from educational patterns, from enculturation and socialising patterns that are no longer relevant. We, the Christ Sparks, working with you, bring into manifestation new forms of relationship that are far more giving of self-respect, that are filled with more integrity and loyalty and love than anything that has yet been experienced.

We have already spoken about the fact that the nature of our form of consciousness is as a swarm. That although we are individual units of consciousness we inter-relate in a way that is totally group self-aware in a way that is naturally and continuously, second by second and present by present, aware of each other's experience. This leads to certain incredibly dynamic modes of pushing forward towards Spirit.

We would like you to imagine us for the moment as a cellular network. Image each cell within this network as having a completely separate and unique consciousness, a completely separate and unique life history, life present and life future. Yet we are all bound together in our acknowledgement and knowing of our unity within the one creative breath that brought us all into being. And we are all bound together within the knowledge that we move in time in the broad sweep of space to a state of pure Spirit. Yet as we pass through time and space through our own forms of self-reflective awareness, we move through moods and states and feelings that are not of pure Spirit, but that resonate with our materialistic base.

Imagine one cell or psyche amongst us brought into resonance with its own materialism. Part of the Spark is resonant with materialism — or egoism. Part of the Spark is resonant with Spirit. In that moment, the Spark feels confusion and friction which takes it into a spin of dissonance. That dissonance echoes out, vibrates out, through the cellular network of which it is a part, **and we are all aware of it**. At the same time that Spark is aware of all of us.

We absorb its confusion while at the same time that Spark absorbs from us our clarity concerning its Spirit. You can see, therefore, that there is virtually no time-lag between its experience of confusion and its experience of our comforting it. They happen simultaneously. We hope that you begin to catch here an understanding of a network of supportive natural love and of open awareness held resonant with higher consciousness.

Imagine that one of the Sparks through its own particular dance and process, becomes blissfully ecstatic in any particular moment. This is immediately connected through the whole of the network and we are all aware of that state with the Spark who is experiencing it. The Spark, in its sanctified and graceful state, blesses all of us simultaneously in the precise moment that it is experiencing its grace. We would like you to recognise the point we made before, that none of this in any way affects or denigrates the individuality of the unique Spark having its own experience. It does however, mean that we are all in that moment when the events are happening, experiencing its experience. The interlinking is intimate and immediate.

Within the occult teaching available to humanity there is a clear notion of the interrelationship and telepathic rapport of all life. But it is not immediate, nor is it cellular in the way that the Christ Sparks exist. The mystic experience, ecstasy, has a form for human. It is like a chalice that **overflows** with the mystical experience and flows out to other people, and is felt *and absorbed by them. This is different from the way in which the Christ Sparks immediately experience, in full, each individual Spark's experience.*

We would like you to understand that the changes happening in humanity at the moment are bringing humanity, or at least the culture which is consciously in resonance with the new metaphysics, into the same form of experience that we the Christ Sparks have.

Now look at where this may manifest at its most intimate. It is within a man and a woman coming together to couple. If they are both in any way upon the Path, and from our perspective there is not one single human being upon the planet who is not upon the Path, they immediately enter the new gestalt which we are bringing into incarnation through the planet. As a couple they are no longer distinct and separate units interacting with each other. We the Sparks have incarnated and seeded into their psyches an instantaneous and mutual empathy of experience.

In the intimacy of coupling, one person's natural spiritual growth — blissful ecstatic experience — is immediately communicated through to the psyche of the partner. There is no differentiation. *But* we cannot help but repeat this over and over again lest we be misunderstood, this does not in any way threaten the uniqueness of the individual personality and identity. At the same time, when one individual in a couple experiences a downward spin or some form of anxiety or depression, this too is instantaneously communicated and experienced by the other. We would like you to appreciate though, that in this form of empathetic experience, we are not talking about the communication of vibrations or the occult communication of energies that can depress. We are talking about empathetic harmony, sympathetic resonance.

We would like to be clearer here: If a woman or a

man comes into a room and is suffering severe depression and is putting out severely depressive vibrations, this may ethero-physically affect everyone else in the room and depress them. When we talk about the instantaneous communication of depression from one member of a couple to the other, we do not mean that form of communication of vibrations. We are talking about a form of *common awareness, a shared experience*.

The unit that is aware of her partner's depression acknowledges it, is empathetic to it, that is all. It is not in itself a bring-down, but what occurs is that the partner can respond by boosting their own love awareness. From our perspective we find this extraordinarily graceful, stimulating and interesting. This love awareness then enters the partner who is depressed, and the partner who is depressed receives a form of illumination. This is an example of one of many hundreds of thousands of inter-relationships that can occur. We are talking here about a form of empathetic sensitivity not previously experienced by human beings. It is similar to the way in which the Angelic realms communicate and experience each other. All this is now possible to human beings because that is how *we* the Sparks experience life. Now we incarnate in you and you share our resonance as well as, subconsciously, our experience. As a friend of William commented, we are like a beneficent virus.

Be aware though that you will not necessarily be conscious of what is happening, either when sharing a high or a low gestalt.

In the esoteric tradition, there was always an ideal that couples should form a spiritual community. But you can see now, from this dynamic form of interrelating in which they can experience themselves as part of a unified cellular consciousness, that the spiritual community that now exists between couples is far more intense and spiritually powerful. At the same time this whole syndrome of mutual empathy and appreciation of position and movement along the path to Spirit provides increasingly difficult problems for the human personality.

We would be very practical here and ask you to imagine a couple who have come together for one or another reasons. They then, in their path through space and time, encounter the Avatar of Synthesis and the Sparks. This could happen through visiting a community, or taking part in some kind of workshop, being influenced by a book, or touching us privately in meditation. It is a huge cultural movement now and we the Sparks are currently touching many hundreds of thousands of people. But look at this couple and the patterns they are carrying. Suddenly, as we observe their psychic experience, they are brought into an intimate form of empathy which they had previously neither worked for nor actively sought or expected. There could be no realistic expectation concerning the experience, because we are an extra-spatial form of consciousness about which this planet was previously totally ignorant. This couple then enters into a new vibrational field and we the Christ Sparks enter into their psyche. They are suddenly drawn into this intimate new form of coupling/dance. It is at this point that a deep level of rhythmic patterning, concerned with each of them as individuals processing along the path, comes to the surface and perhaps demonstrates the inappropriateness of their coupling. By the old laws — by the old reasons, rationalisations and justifications it may seem absolutely perfect that they should be together. However as we the Sparks enter into their psyches and draw them into the new forms of consciousness and empathy, it becomes apparent to the couple that their mutual process is no longer harmonious. Their rhythms become dissonant, there is mutual alienation and they ask why this should be so.

You may demand a bit of logical clarity concerning why, when we enter in the field of consciousness of any couple, this does not, in fact, provoke a form of greater mutual support. That may indeed happen, but what we cannot cure and heal are deep-seated incarnational patterns which exist in individual human beings. We can bring a couple into empathic rapport with one another and certainly, no matter how badly they get on, they can, if they choose to invoke the energies of pure Christed spirit and the will-to-grow, melt themselves into a resonant accord which is appropriate to their new empathy. But for many couples this is asking too much. They have their own deep-seated rhythms and patterns of growth and change and the two people can no longer move hand in hand. It is as if one of them is running and one of them is skipping. Or in another couple, it is as if one of them may be happy doing a stomach crawl along the grass while carefully examining everything in the way, while the other one wishes to catch a hang-glider. In those kinds of situations, the empathy that we bring between the two of them means that they must part. They might previously have been totally compatible in terms of culture, intellect and social well-being, but our effect upon them may be to accelerate them into changes that demonstrate the inappropriateness of the relationship.

Equally, when couples are brought into rapport with each other because of us, they can experience an extremely intense form of spiritual growth and psychological insight. This is because, if they surrender to the empathy that we bring about between them, they can find a form of bonding and safe affection. This gives them the most profound type of psychological security which allows them to accept lessons and insights which were hitherto forbidden. These forbidden lessons would have been too threatening to their psychological well- being and tranquillity.

Session Four. 17th August 1987

I'm back in London and still uncertain within myself whether the source which is channelling is myself or something external. I've noticed myself trying to second-guess what is going to be written next and wondering whether I am working on writing it myself.

We wish to continue now with our discussion of how our penetration of human psyches and human auras has affected the way in which relationships are conducted between couples.

We have already expressed that once we incarnate into the psyches of a couple, they begin to work and relate together in a far more intense form of empathetic rapport. They begin to function psychically as two cells within the same form of organism. They act as two clear identities, yet within one gestalt. They need not be conscious of this at all. We shall pursue this matter of identities, personalities, within the implications of this for larger groups later on.

We want to discuss couples first because there is an urgency in your culture for clarity about the problems in contemporary relationships. The question continually put forward is: 'What are the rules in a relationship?'

The rules are, and always have been, that people should develop spiritually, yet with responsibility for the environment within which they exist and function.

The primary responsibility of each individual — whether in a relationship or not — is to spiritually evolve. That does not stop when someone comes into a relationship. The purpose of a relationship is to enhance a person's spiritual evolution. This may seem obvious, but all too often individuals who are self-conscious walkers upon the Path, move into a relationship and regress into primal forms of self-pity, distress and selfishness. This totally blocks their using the relationship for any form of evolution. They wallow in a state which is solely part of their own history and karma and project the reasons for the unpleasant experience on to their partner.

We would state as firmly as we possibly can that before readers can fully understand the dimensions that we the Sparks bring into relationship patterns, they must first of all put their house in order. This means that when in a relationship or entering a relationship, they must be totally clear that the relationship is not to be a foggy and confused environment for displays of resistant personality karma and egocentrism. Relationships are opportunities for growth, love and support.

Readers, equally, cannot duck the fact that they are ecologically responsible for their environment and should care for it with sensitive awareness. Within a relationship the immediate environment is your partner. The immediate ecological responsibility you have — for the nearest life-form — is your partner. Individuals in couples must be ecologically aware of the vibrations that they put out which affect their partner.

It is in vogue at the moment for women and men of the industrial culture to discuss the ecological needs of the planet as a whole, with particular reference to the effects of greedy industrialised humans upon the mineral, vegetable and animal realms. Often in the media, you will read about the rape of the earth, about the misuse of the plant kingdom and the desecration of the animal kingdom. This is fine — but again, it points out the human pattern of ignoring the crucial human relations which, to say the least, are also a part of the general ecology — and the closest.

Again, we stress that within a relationship the individual's primary ecological responsibility is to their partner.

This requires a sensitive and caring attitude. It also requires, in the same way that human beings draw in their horns when it comes to raping the earth or using too much of the earth's resources or when being greedy, that you draw in your horns — be careful — with your partner. In fact, one can clearly state that it is with your partner in a relationship that you should attempt to be on your very best ecological behaviour.

If two people come together with this form of understanding and mutual respect that each other's primary purpose is to evolve spiritually and that their primary and immediate ecological responsibility is for each other, then you have the crucial foundation stones for a healthy, self-respecting and in many ways ecstatic relationship.

What we have just described are the rules which have always applied to the way in which a woman and a man should join together for a long-term relationship. The contemporary situation has been dramatically intensified by our own incarnation over the last twenty-five years and by our increasing infiltration into the psyches and auras of humanity.

We should state here that the awareness which we bring will, sooner or later be incarnate across the planet in all humanity. This will bring problems just as much as it brings blessings. Humanity as a whole and individually, still has to work out its own karma.

As we incarnate into the psyches of individuals we bring men and women in relationships into that new empathetic rapport with each other. We bring a form of mutual resonance which creates a single auric field around them. This means that the atmosphere which is created by them is intensified and amplified, as is the radiation from their auric field.

A couple must be self-conscious and reflective, both individually and in conversation together, about what it is that they are putting out into their environment. This is not simply to state that they should be aware that after having argued or made love, of what it is that they are vibrating out to the planet. We are not talking about those forms of obvious vibrational effects but the general auric and magnetic effect that a couple has. This is more subtle but also more deeply affecting. We are asking couples to be self-reflective about the nature of the resonance which the synergy and alchemical fusion of their relationship bring about. Couples should recognise that they spend an immense amount of time together, more than they do with anyone else, if only by their bodies sleeping together at night. Two people living together create a gestalt which is more than the sum of their individual lives put together.

We are suggesting, therefore, that couples should reflect upon the nature of the synergetic atmosphere they express to their environment. We are actually asking for couples to stop, pause and communicate together about this on a daily basis. We are talking here about couples *attuning together*.

In the same way that many of you are meditating on a daily basis, or are taking silence together in communities on a daily or weekly basis, we are now talking about couples also attuning together on a daily basis. They can attune to their relationship and take spiritual responsibility in a way that is in resonance with the changes of our time. We do not think we need to spell this out further. We think it self-evidently creative and constructive for couples to work in this way. The benefits, in terms of a more responsible attitude both to themselves as individuals, to themselves as a couple and to their environment, are obvious. Moreover, this form of daily attunement and careful awareness to what it is that they are creating together will bring about a psychological fluidity and an emotional goodwill. This helps to melt many of the emotional and mental difficulties which couples experience.

Many have commented upon the fact that the last two decades have seen a time of 'Dispensation' in terms of the fast psychological liberation that can be brought to people through the new forms of therapy. This is particularly true with the therapies associated with the humanistic and transpersonal movements. We would also like to mention that a couple of synthetic drugs were manifested in the last two decades which have about them the energy of Dispensation if they are used in a sacred and holy manner.

We would like to point out that this Dispensation *is available to couples* if they have the discipline to regularly make use of the opportunities which are available to them now through the incarnation of the Avatar of Synthesis and the Christ Sparks. If couples attune themselves, they will place themselves in resonance with the rapidly approaching general Christ energies. These are accelerating the general melting process of the materialistic and painful patterns which in the past have caused awful growth difficulties. There is the opportunity now for couples to melt through many of these past patterns of anger, pain, self-pity and repressed hurts and injuries, from the past, from this life-time and from previous lives.

The rules for relationships are really quite simple. We shall repeat some of the statements we have just made and add nuances we think are relevant:

> **First,** couples should come together with respect for each other's individual spiritual growth.

> **Second,** couples should come together with an awareness that each individual takes ecological responsibility for how he/she affects his/her partner. Your partner is your major environmental responsibility.

Third, couples should be aware of what it is they synergetically emanate from their auras as a couple — and be aware of this by taking daily attunement and by reflecting together upon it.

Fourth, couples should be aware of the fact that they work together to melt through the patterns of both partners. There is no point in being in the intense vortex of a coupling situation unless you take the opportunity to work consciously and with discipline on melting your own inert and regressive patterns. This requires strength, courage and honesty about your own individual shortcomings, and an expansive attitude of affection and support for your partner.

We can imagine you asking about when relationships start to go wrong. We can present no general rules for when and how relationships should either begin or end. We would state, however, that in terms of beginnings we would ask only that couples approach each other always within an atmosphere of intuitive knowing that their coupling is appropriate and that they come together, instinctively and physically, with affection. In terms of endings, we understand fully that there are immense and painful problems involved here. We are saying, however, that if couples would bother on a daily basis to attune together and to discuss what it is that they are synergetically emanating — and as they do this to melt through the emotional and lower mental hooks that bind them painfully to each other — that they will be able to move in a more graceful manner into the future.

It is not what individuals do, but how they *be* that matters. When they die and look back through their lives, what they notice is a wake, a history of moods, not actions. Look at the history of what you emanated to your environment and what you as individuals emanated to each other. Look back at your radiation, not at your actions.

We play sparkfully through you. Do you not see that it is all changed, all changing? We love you. We love everyone and everything. We are Sparks working with the Christ.

End of session.

~~~~

(The following extract was dictated two months later and was originally in the section concerned with cosmic relationships. However, it seems more appropriate to place it here.)

We acknowledge however that the nature of these exercises — a couple daily attuning and talking together about what they, as individuals and together, radiate — can intensify the psychological difficulties between two people. It forces them to address each other in an intimate way which can spiral into difficult psychic atmospheres as much as into good ones and as we the Sparks become more aware and attuned to the human condition we realise that we ourselves may be innocent and naive in our expectations. We lack a certain sense of realism about the nature of human emotional life.

It may be, though, that what we lack in realism, you the readers of this book, lack in disciplined detachment and a sense of harmonious centredness. We wonder and are surprised more and more by the profound alienation that human beings have from their beingness, both in a cosmic and planetary sense. By planetary sense we refer not only to the individual human within the vast space that is the planet but also the individual human being simply within the three-dimensional space that exists within a few yards around him at any given moment. We would ask each reader of this book, at this precise second, to pause as you read and to experience how you relate to your immediate surroundings — the air, the space around you. Do you have any relationship with it? Do you know where you are? Do you know who you are? Do you know how you are?

4

Groups, Communities and Politics

This is the 21st August 1987. It's ten to nine in the morning. I'm in the flat. I have no idea what this session is about.

The title of this section is "Groups, Communities and Politics."

We have described the manner in which our incarnation affects and dynamises the empathetic intimacies in the relationships of couples. In the same manner we work to dynamise the empathetic and intuitive intimacies between more than two people when they come together for a specific purpose. To be clear, we encourage the specific purpose to have an aspect of overt self-conscious spirituality to it.

It should be recognised, when people come together to work on any particular project, that the project itself is not the crucial form with which they are operating. The essence of the operation, when any group works together, is the synergy* that they themselves create. This may seem contradictory, for when a group of people come together to build a house, or to bring any project into fruition, it appears overtly that the house or the project is

---

*Synergy: The loving enhancement and amplification of any energy situation that occurs when energies cooperate and synthesise — particularly human energies.

the goal. This is not the case. It is but the manifestation of an idea to which the group is temporarily attached.

The idea or the project may well be one that manifests itself in terms of service, but this service is just a useful coincidence. There are many things which individuals and groups do which are of service to the community and in these cases the work is itself a form of yoga. But what we are concerned with here, is the essence — the inner life or subjectivity — of the project upon which the people are working.

It is a standard cliche of esoteric teaching that all form is but the manifestation of an inner idea. All magical work is based on the understanding that it is the subjective world of ideas which precipitates manifestation, appearance and form. Therefore, when we suggest that it is not the building of a house, or the completion of a project, which is the essence, but that the inner aspects of it are the crucial dimension, we say nothing new.

We wish to emphasise, however, that form does not come first and the inner dimension second. The inner dimension is first and the manifestation second.

Nothing can be built, constructed or brought into fruition, unless it is previously worked upon in thought and in imagination. Just because the process then moves into a dimension in which the project manifests in a three-dimensional form, because it can be touched, smelled, heard, seen and tasted, does not mean that its multi-dimensionality, from the world of inner ideas, has disappeared into the simplicity of material manifestation. Just as the work was conceived out of thought and imagination, so the dynamics of thought and imagination — the inner dynamics — continue through the structure and fulfilment of the form.

When a group comes together to create and build something, it is — as with a coupling relationship — the atmosphere, the mood that they create as they work, which is crucial.

In many communities, any form of group work is preceded by moments of attunement. The purpose of these short moments of silence is to bring the group members into harmony with each other and into harmony with the purpose of the shared work. The attunement of the group members facilitates the work being done more harmoniously and more in resonance with the inner meaning of the work. Most groups, as soon as they begin to work, lose the sense of multi-dimensionality of that which they are doing and enter into a form of consciousness that is focussed only upon the three-dimensional materialistic form which they are constructing. We are concerned here to emphasise that — despite the fact that the hands may indeed be moving hammer on to nail, fingers on to keyboard and so on — what is happening in essence, in the true multi-dimensional reality, is a process of thought and imagination. This is the case whether or not the workers are self-conscious and aware of this process.

It has certainly been the ideal of all spiritual communities and groups to work with an awareness of the spiritual harmony required second by second regardless of what is actually being done. It is also part of the New Age ideology that individuals, when they work together in groups, discipline themselves and surrender their personalities to a form of group harmony. With the incarnation of the Avatar of Synthesis the nature of group work has been intensely dynamised. The opportunity exists now for individuals who are working together in groups to become aware of a rapport and synergy between them which has not previously been available.

The reality of contemporary group work is such that it is now possible for groups to move with great speed through processes which would previously have taken many years to melt, through friction, the personality problems of distrust, isolation and fear between individual members. If we use the Masonic symbolism of Building the Temple — especially the symbolism of smoothing down all unnecessary roughage from the stones which are to make the Temple, it is now possible for Temples to be constructed — Temples of Harmonious Group Activity — with a hundred times the speed than was previously possible. Groups can choose to come together and put themselves into a state of instantaneous Christed harmony.

This is possible because the nature of our incarnation into the psyches of human beings is such that they are placed, as we stated earlier, into a form of immediate empathetic rapport. If they are prepared to move in a style of surrendered and trusting dance together, they will find they can pass forward through space and time in a fast, Christed harmony that will astonish the group, that will bring them a form of ecstatic bliss and peace. There are already groups which have experienced this form of working together.

We are suggesting that, where individual members are prepared to put this amount of spiritual awareness and discipline into their attitude when they come to work within a group, they should indeed do so and not be distracted.

When individuals come into group work, they should prepare themselves *in advance* to be dynamically interrelated to the people with whom they are working. We are not talking about the speed of the actual physical work. The last thing we are asking for is any rushes of adrenaline or flows of fast physical energy into bringing any project into completion. We are asking for a form of dynamic acceleration in terms of *psychic attitude*. We are asking people to open themselves up to real group experience. Imagine for a moment that you have a zipper running up your aura from your feet to a point above your heads. From the bottom upwards undo the zipper and open yourself to the group psyche with which you are working. This may sound threatening to sensitive souls who day by day are accustomed to putting up defenses in order to retain a modicum of stability in a world which appears frightening and aggressive. Most of the people in the New Age movement think they are sensitive souls. We are telling you, that it is now possible for you sensitive souls to open yourselves up to group work and to suffer no damage other than having to change. Take off your armour. Do not hold back. It is no longer necessary to keep up these forms of defence. In fact, given the nature of the inner dynamic which now exists upon the planet, it is a form of inertia, a form of blasphemy, to hold back from opening up to the group with which you are working.

We are suggesting, with sensitivity to the pain and difficulties you have experienced in the past, that it is possible for you to be completely open, in your own private and discrete manner, to the group members with whom you are working. We are not suggesting any enthusiastic emotionalism with people — no athletic confession! We assume that the people who are reading this material are disciplined spiritual workers, prepared to use their adult intelligence and life experience in a mature and considered way. Opening up can only be sensibly achieved by those of you who know, from your meditations and daily awareness, what are the problems of processing change, and what struggles exist in opening up and in being honest with yourself.

Imagine the immense wonder and excitement that could exist in a group of very mature and adult human beings who come together with this attitude. Imagine a group of women and men coming together to build a house, to fulfil a certain project. Before they come into the group, each one of them, in their morning meditation, affirms to herself that in the day to come, "I am open. I am open to the experience, in synergy, of my fellow workers. From Earth to Heaven, I surrender to the Christed Spirit of our work and I recognise the synergy of our process. I do this carefully, with strength and with trust."

Now imagine that each and every worker coming together on a project affirms these words or something similar to themselves before they come to the work. Imagine that when they actually come together and hold hands or form a circle of attunement, that each individual — privately again — affirms that recognition. We are not suggesting here for one moment that there be some form of group imposition about how this affirmation should be manifest in the group. We are saying that each individual, in her or his personal privacy, may decide that mode of operation should be her approach. We suggest that individuals can hold that attitude within groups even when it is not shared by others. If just one person in a group will adopt that mode of working, then he or she can have great influence for silent good upon the other members.

Now, imagine that the whole group has focussed on that way of working. They come together. They attune, each of them with a private awareness that that is how they wish to be with each other — and then imagine them passing through the day working together. The work gets completed as usual, but here we have a situation in which each individual has privately taken responsibility, has privately affirmed their awareness, for the synergy of the group as it works through the day. This is an adult and mature method of spiritual work in the new age. It will evoke a form of grounded harmony and bliss in the participants. Such rhythms of working together *go forward through decades and centuries* and become a mode of approaching all work and all life.

This harmony and bliss is now available because of the nature of our incarnation into the psyches of individuals. The empathetic, intuitive relationships now possible between people are in harmony with the incarnating Christ Spirit of the Cosmos now infiltrating through into this planet. We bring a sense of fruition and calm. We bring a sense of the cellular solidarity of humans working together. This is in resonance with the most pure creative and constructive harmonics of manifestation in the universe.

We can, therefore, suggest that as with couples, there are certain rules that individuals in group work can apply:

> **One**, before coming into group work, privately make an attunement and affirmation similar to the one we have suggested above.

> **Two,** each individual in any group work must be aware that, as they pass through the time and space involved in the work, their major process is not the completion of the work itself, but their own spiritual progress — and the spiritual progress of the other members of the group.

> **Three,** each participant in group work has to be aware of her/his spiritual responsibility to the group ecological environment. Their immediate ecological environment is the other group members and they have responsibility towards them. What are you emanating, in terms of psychic ecology, to the other members of the group?

> **Four**, the members of the group, individually and later as a group in the form of conscious attunement, must be aware of the synergetic aura which they are putting out. It would seem

appropriate that groups involved in any form of work should take time occasionally to discuss what it is that they are radiating. This can happen casually over sandwiches at lunchtime or cups of tea. We suggest that the atmosphere for this kind of a conversation be kept relaxed and friendly, not formalised into a group circle led by a chairperson, except in situations of difficulty and disharmony which may require a more disciplined focus. We are suggesting that humanity enjoys itself.

End of that session, William. Thank you.

~~~~

This is Sunday 23rd of August. Its ten to six in the evening. I would like to mention that I was personally quite impressed by the last two sessions and am beginning to feel more accepting of this whole process.

Now that we have spent some time discussing the nature of relationships in couples and groups, we would like to pass on to the more complex and complicated subject of the effect of he Avatar of Synthesis and the Christ Sparks upon communities. By communities we initially refer to small communities of anything from one hundred and fifty people upwards, through to larger political communities — from villages to nation-states — and finally the world community.

It is obvious when we are discussing communities of this size that the nature of the interaction between the individuals cannot be as intimate as that between individuals in couples and small groups. It is not possible for the attunement that can happen in small groupings to occur on the scale of societies. This is not to say that it is not desirable and, to a degree, it can indeed happen.

In the West, for example, national communities do pause and attune together. In a weekly rhythm, national communities tend to pause and take a breathing space on Sundays, particularly Sunday mornings. People who are aware of the inner dynamic of relationships can, in their meditations, take advantage of these Sunday morning spaces to magically work with and create a more electric-dynamic network of consciousness through their communities. It is possible to tune into and recognise the need of the community members — village, street, town, nation, continent — on a Sunday morning for a period of quiet and attunement for a nurturing of their creaturehood. The individual meditator can imagine a blanket of energy interconnecting all the members of their society. As the meditator tunes into these connections, he or she can amplify the nurture and calm absorbed by the community. This amplification is created by the self-conscious awareness with which he or she plugs into the network. Thus a great synergy is created and a more powerful synergetic aura is radiated.

Here we draw an exact parallel between the synergetic aura created by couples or by small groups with that created by a larger community or society. The larger society, however, cannot pause and become self-aware of its activities. This is so simply because the society is too large for overt group intercommunication to take place between all members — although covert communication does, of course, take place at an intuitive and telepathic level.

It is possible, however, for the individual — the spiritual and meditative worker — to create and amplify the telepathic energy links between the units, to network them and to build in his/her own awareness a consciousness of the synergetic aura of that society.

It is possible to work in this manner not simply with communities who exist in specific geographical spaces — such as a nation-state or a village or a spiritual community — but also with specific groups of people within a community. For example, many subjectively aware Christian workers connect, in meditation, with the network of Christian worship happening simultaneously. Thus, they tune into — and amplify — the cellular psyche of Christians working in silence and in Spirit upon Sunday mornings.

In the same way that meditators can consciously work to interweave the energies of the national or local community, they can also work with the energies of all the various forms of celebration and religious practice. Meditators can interweave and interconnect them, and become aware of the synergetic aura that exists — and reinforce and amplify it. It is possible to do this work with all religious groups. Jewish groups, for instance, may do it on Friday and Saturday mornings. Moslems may do it, if they wish to, at the various times of prayer during the day, and at their spiritual festivals throughout the year, such as Ramadan. It is possible to do this kind of work with all the world religions.

This magical work amplifies the synergetic aura of communities, following the basic principle that energy follows thought. The meditator, in becoming aware of the network of interrelationships in any community — religious, cultural or geographical — actually helps to build and create the lines of energy networking the cells that are the units of that community. If you live in a small village — or road or block of apartments — and on a Sunday morning you become aware of the various families and individuals in that community taking a pause, getting up late, reading the Sunday papers, generally having a relaxed and easy time— if you become aware of the individuals behaving in this way and become aware then of their interrelationship, you actually create their subjective community. You facilitate them becoming a community seeking calm and nurture on a Sunday morning — whether they are conscious of it or not. As you become aware of them, you actively place energy into their system and amplify the subjective connections between individuals.

It is important to do this work from a meditative space which is balanced, detached and non-interfering. The attitude is one of pure and loving awareness. It is not one that in any way radiates energy from the meditator's physical body; no strain or dynamic energy is experienced.

There have been various meditation movements since the last war which have been intuitively aware of this whole process. They have advertised the fact that if there were a certain number of meditators in any particular area, this would have a radiatory affect which would bring peace to the area. This is indeed true. We, however, are suggesting that the meditators take it a step further and instead of simply being channels and radiators of harmonic energies, they become magic weavers of the cellular interconnections between the people who live within the community.

By amplifying the connections between the individual psyches within the community in a way that is aware of the spiritual nurturing aspect of their interrelationship, one then amplifies that particular aspect of the community relationships to a very powerful degree. Of course, this kind of awareness can be used for rabble-rousing — and in the past groups have done this in a wicked occult fashion. We would like to affirm for you that the nature of the the Avatar of Synthesis and of our incarnation, the Christ Sparks, into the psyches and auras of indi-

viduals upon the planet, means that the kind of evil networking done in the past is becoming increasingly difficult to achieve.

Now, we would like to make explicit exactly what
we are suggesting to you. By doing this form of medita-
tional work, by becoming aware of and actually amplifying the cellular interconnection between units of consciousness that make up a community, we are talking
about strengthening the peaceful and loving synergetic
aura of any community or society of beings. The natures
of the incarnating Christ energies, the Avatar of Synthesis and our own incarnation, allow this kind of work to
invoke and draw Christed atmospheres and energies into
the mass psyche of the community. This work is not simply one that builds upon the Christ Within or the aspiration to peaceful divinity within the psyches of the members of the community.

The inner structure of the total psyche of humanity
is such at the moment that if you consciously work in this
way, to network individuals, you are quietly invoking the
incarnation of the available energies of peaceful divinity
into the community. Done on a daily and weekly basis,
on an ongoing rhythm that goes on into the future through
the years to come you may effect miraculous changes
within your communities.

We are not suggesting that you do this work in such
a manner that it resembles a form of intense prayer that
invokes the energies of some higher and mysterious
divinity. We suggest that you work with an understanding that by simply accepting these ideas you will emanate
and radiate the new energies of Christed peace, and synergy and group consciousness.

Simply by sitting in silence and networking, by
doing that in a harmonic peace, you will create your own
local communal and harmonic convergence. We would
entreat you to work in this way.

It is possible to work on an extraordinarily large scale in this manner. Certain groups and disciples will wish to work on a scale which recognises the community of the global society, and in these situations, you may work in two ways. Either bring to your awareness the natural networks of human beings connecting countries at various levels, such as international statesmen and women, people working through the agencies of goodwill such as the Red Cross, tourists, business people, airline pilots and so on. Or you can work directly with the psyches — 'folk souls' — of individual nations.

We would like you to play with, in your imagination, various groups that you can imagine. See these groups manifesting and networking with their new radiatory synergetic aura.

If you yourself are a politician or a decision-maker involved in political work with groups, please pause daily and become aware of all the things which we have just discussed. Be aware of your cellular interconnection with the group within which you are working, especially your political opponents. We would like to emphasise the fact that there is absolutely nothing inappropriate or wrong with political argument and with creative discussion in which opposing views come together. The whole nature of aggressive argument leading to a synthetic outcome is one which we applaud.

Argument, however, must include an acceptance in goodwill of the intimate relationship with opposing ideas. If, on a daily basis, politicians across the planet were to sit in silent attunement and be aware of the constructive intimacy of their relationship with their political opponents there would be a profound change in many of their actions.

That is enough for this session. We do not wish to overload you. Thank you. We end at twelve minutes past six.

*This is the 15th August and its nine twenty-six.
I have them right there at the top of my head.*

We would like to continue our discussion about the nature of the effect of our incarnation and the Avatar of Synthesis in the world of relationships, particularly between couples, small groups and communities.

We have already spent a while discussing the profound effect it would have upon political relationships if the individual actors in the political scene realised that, along with their colleagues and opponents, they are co-creators in the reality in which they are working. As co-creators, their political antagonists are to be *honoured* as players within the same field. Such an attitude, however, requires a certain level of detachment which is not yet to be found among politicians, nor will it be found in the foreseeable future. This is not to say that conscious esoteric workers cannot create the networking form, the helpful synergetic aura which will in the end bring about this form of peace between political antagonists.

We are looking here for an understanding of political realities that was glimpsed in the Platonic and Aristotelian visions two thousand years ago, but was then merely an idea which intellects of a high order could experience. Their teachings, though uttered repeatedly day by day over centuries, have been learnt only in an ideological and intellectual fashion but have hardly been experienced. This is because of the nature of the aura of the planet and because humanity's karma was such as to not allow the incarnation of that ideal. We, however, are stating that it is possible for that ideal — the joy of argument leading to decision-making — to begin to incarnate into experience. The essence of harmful political conflict is not in the opposing viewpoints, but in the psychological attitudes of the people arguing. Politics is not the problem.

The problem is the politicians. It is not the argument, but the arguers.

As previously discussed, in the networking that can take place on a national and global scale by individual esoteric workers working in moments of community silence such as Sunday mornings, meditators do not simply create a telepathic network between individuals. They precipitate into incarnation the whole nature of the synergetic aura which we are bringing into humanity. We now suggest that this form of work be augmented by meditators, individually or in groups, focussing upon the creation of a series of ideas, in particular *the joyful creativity of political conflict.*

This mode of approaching political conflict can completely change the attitude of the observers who currently, from their 'new age' perspective, look with judgementalism upon the way politics is conducted. We suggest that the political scene *not* be impregnated with unrealistic ideas/thought-forms of peace or harmonious government, but that the various arenas of political conflict be infused with a perceptive and insightful attitude concerning the playful and joyful creativity which is taking place within the decision-making. What people outside the political game must understand is that it is goodwill and a desire to serve which inspires political participants. What is not happening at the moment, however, is any sense of this joyful movement into the future manifesting in conflicts. What is required for a peaceful solution to political conflicts, both on a small and large scale, is a fusion of a creative and happy attitude into the whole process.

We are, therefore, stating as clearly as we can, that meditation work done to affect political conflict should focus on enfusing it with *humorous sportsmanship.* This is inherent, for example, in the political ideals which overlight the British Houses of Parliament and the various democratic forms of governments which have been inspired by the Westminster model.

This political ideal, as well as hovering over the psyches of the participants, is now capable of actual incarnation into the hearts and daily experiences of the political actors.

To move from a macro to a micro perspective, you can also see how this perspective on political conflict can be applied to couples. Alongside the daily contemplation and awareness of the synergetic aura a couple manifests in the world, they might also look at the conflict that takes place between them as a form of co-creative decision-making for the way they move into the future. The problems that exist between them are not points of friction but points of undulation as they pass through time. In the same way that a surfer flows fast down a curve of waves and then bounces across them, so couples can also regard their arguments.

This same interpretation and attitude also applies, of course, to small group decision-making. How many times do you get frustrated by group decision-making and personal conflict? Let the conflict become playful in you. Do not tell anyone else to be playful. Let it begin solely in you and let it begin in the spirit of silence.

With the incarnation of the Christ Sparks and the Avatar of Synthesis, and the approaching closeness of the Christ energies, it is time for the wallowing self-reflection upon inner conflict to be replaced by a joyful understanding that all conflict is the manifestation of human beings correctly passing through time. It is impossible for people to pass through time without experiencing conflict. The problem is not in noticing conflict, but in ignoring or repressing the awareness of it. We would ask you to change your attitude to the way in which you do notice conflict. Do not judge it. Do not attempt to make it disappear. Fill it with Love.

5

More Groups

In this brief section, we wish to bring you fully into resonance with ideas concerning the number of groups of which you are a member. You belong to more groups than you can perhaps imagine.

Recognising that there is a magnetic attraction between objects which vibrate with a similar resonance, you can choose to become aware of the different ways in which you vibrate. How many different aspects are there to your character and personality? Each of these aspects forms a group, at a subjective and telepathic level, with all the other aspects which are of a similar resonance. Human beings are not simply members of groups to which they obviously belong. This is common knowledge to people with any spiritual education, for they recognise that all human personalities are manifestations of an inner soul which has a history of connections that make for distinct inner groups.

There are, however, many more subjective groups, telepathically and intuitively linked, which exist at a personality level of consciousness. Although they exist at this level, you will not be aware of them, but they are very real, quite dynamic and have a definite effect upon their environment. As an exercise you might choose, with pen and paper, to list the number of aspects that belong to your personality. In the exercise that William conducts, people usually come up with about twenty aspects of their personality: the parent, the lover, the bohemian, the sportsperson and so on. It is fairly obvious that, at an inner

level, all very sporty people - due to a similarity in resonance - form a distinct group. They emanate into humanity as a whole a particular atmosphere. In many ways this
atmosphere - because of its health enhancing facets - is
beneficent. In other ways, for example in its atmosphere
of competitiveness, it may not be so helpful.

If you have a competitive nature, you can imagine
that you form a resonant whole with others who have a
competitive nature. Within your workplace, be aware that
if you do have a competitive personality, you form a distinct group with all the others who are also competitive.
One aspect of your mind might wish to reject this information for we are suggesting that you form a group with
your *competitors*, the people to whom you may be antag-
onistic. However, from the perspective of the whole workplace, you and your fellow competitors form a distinct
group emanating a distinct atmosphere into the workplace. You may not be able to effect any changes in the
rest of the group, but it is best to be aware of your role
and what you radiate. You cannot duck taking responsibility for that which you radiate.

Equally, you may be a non-assertive and timid person, and therefore will form a group with all those types
as well. Is what you emanate constructive? Are you aware
of it? It might be possible to start an explicit group for all
your fellows to discuss and help clear your group timid-
ity. Indeed this happens informally in some workplaces.

If you are a clerk, you form a part of a planetary
groups of clerks. If you are a salesperson, you form a part
of a planetary group of sales people. You can see, therefore, that at different levels and in different aspects, you
form interlinking, interrelating, complex patterns of relationship - locally and globally - with all the various aspects
of what you are. *This is true for everyone*. No one is
excluded. The aggressive business executive in his Wall
Street suite is in direct relationship with the aggressive

seven year old Chinese girl demanding a new silk dress for her doll. There are no separations.

People are connected with people. Frequently, if individuals were to understand clearly who it is that they are in group relationship with, they would be extremely embarrassed.

The ramifications of all this are quite interesting for those who are prepared to ponder on this in their meditations and contemplations. In each distinct field of connection, in each distinct group, it is possible to take responsibility and to know that, second by second, you play your full part in the kaleidoscope of manifestation which is human life upon this planet.

Through these various energy connections, all individuals, via their groups, are *culturally* interlinked. There are no individuals or groups which exist in isolation of any kind. This is not to deny either the uniqueness of specific cultures or individuals. It is only to point out that energy swims, dances and resonantly vibrates between all living beings upon the planet.

At the top of the business pyramid sits the chief executive, apparently alone in her/his decision-making power. This is the boss. Look just for a minute into the more subtle dimensions and you will see the various connections between that individual and other individuals within the pyramid. There are also connections with others all across the planet. How are they linked? Catch the various energy threads. There may be a thread of insecurity related to the opposite sex which binds that individual to millions of others.

This way of perceiving things brings all people into an awareness that you are living beings who are part of the one single unit, which is life upon this planet.

We would ask you then to be careful about yourselves and to ignore no part of your character. Humans cannot afford to be negligent about what they really are.

All too often people, especially within the metaphysical, new age culture, examine carefully everything except themselves. What we are suggesting is a careful and shrewd examination of yourselves using all the intelligence and insight that you have. Be aware of the resonance and emanation of each aspect. Look at it all and know yourself. You may if you choose, in meditation, spend some time examining the different inner aspects of yourself, examining the groups with which these aspects are linked and examining what you radiate.

And be always aware that through love, you are connected with everything.

End of session.

6

Healing

This is the 27th of August. The time is 11.20 at night. We're in the flat in London. I had an interesting experience earlier today of feeling and being fully aware of the Sparks — or the resonance of the Sparks — incarnate through my whole body. It was a very high, beautiful sensation. It only lasted a few seconds. It was a glimpse of a reality that could last longer. Anyway we shall see what they have for us in this session.

This is the beginning of a new chapter. We would like to discuss in detail the forms of healing in which we are involved and to clarify the nature of the new forms of healing — particularly psychological — which are now available. Essentially the greater part of disease is the result of psychological turmoil — unconscious conflict between the inner purpose of the incarnating consciousness and the outer expression/action of the personality.

When the behaviour of the personality is in dissonance with the purpose of the inner being, the resulting disharmony manifests in a form of energy convulsion in the aura of the vehicle, which anchors in the vehicle itself. You then have a physical manifestation of that inner energy convulsion — illness.

This is not said in the judgment that people are or can be — second by second, day by day, or year by year

— responsible for their illnesses. We do not like the insensitive and harsh ideology in which the individual alone is responsible for her own illness. This is the, "it's your creation" mentality. It may appear to be the case but ignores the astonishing length of history which precedes any particular human being's existence now this moment in time and space. As we said earlier, one of the great lessons for us the Sparks, as we understand life upon this planet, is the *hard* effect that time has on people. Time is the dimension through which you pass in order to effect the changes from a space of — it is difficult to find the correct word here because we mean no value judgment — of imperfection to perfection. This is merely expressed, however, in the *dimension* of time. It is not the reality in the dimensions that transcend time. We transcend time and, therefore, have had difficulties in understanding the exact process through which human beings pass. In coming to understand it, it has brought to us and our own experience a depth of sensitivity which we find full of growth.

Although dis-ease and illness are the manifestation of a dissonance between inner purpose and outer expression, it is simplistic to wish for a situation in which any human being can perfectly express outwardly their inner purpose. The human being who can do this, has brought her personality expression into a space that transcends time. This person is, by your terms of reference, a perfected being.

This is to remind you of the deeper philosophical and practical implications of karma. All human beings bring their past history into their present. To put it another way, one can say that all human beings have, in the very fabric of their personality structure — here we are talking again about their physical, emotional and mental make-up — a history and resonance of materialism which is dissonant with the purpose of inner self. Remember what we described before about the nature of the incarnating inner spirit and the fact that the human personality is made up of energy-matter-consciousness that belongs to a previous and different resonance.

It is, therefore, to be expected that human beings endure and experience illness and disease. The problem is not so much with the disease itself and its manifestation, but with the attitude of the individual to the disease. There are several insightful presentations being made at the moment which are precisely concerned with bringing the creative aspects of disease to people's awareness. The creativity of illness lies precisely in the fact that illness is such an overt manifestation of the clash between the purpose of the inner self and the personality, that the consciousness of the individual, mediating between the two, has no choice but to come to an awareness of that clash. The clash cannot now be ignored. Well, it is less easy to ignore.

People live their lives in a state of dissonance without being aware of it. What illness does is to bring such an obvious projection of the dissonance into manifestation that they cannot avoid the issue.

Illness then presents an overt and timely reminder of inner dissonance. It presents the sick person with a practically unavoidable opportunity for change. We are talking here about changing patterns of behaviour. Do you sincerely want to change? We are talking here about changing immensely long historical threads of attitude, vibration and rhythmic expression in your incarnations. This is not easy.

The modern movement of psychology has done much to reveal the hidden layers of psychological reality which affect behaviour. These layers are normally hidden in unconsciousness. It is, however, limiting to understand these layers as being restricted to this life.

What has all this to do with the Sparks?

Our resonance brings into the general psychic field

of humanity the opportunity for immensely rapid changes of past patterns into new forms of being resonant with the harmonics of the Cosmic Christ. We present here the opportunities not only to transcend profoundly difficult historic patterns, but also the possibility to re-energise and revibrate them in a form that has never been known on this planet before. We are also talking about new modes of healing and change which can, in a few short hours, affect transitions which might previously have taken life-times. How can this be so?

We would first draw your attention to the introduction of therapies in the last two decades which have facilitated the spiritual and psychological evolution of disciples, particularly the gestalt, humanistic and transpersonal schools of psychology. Those of you who have experienced the healing associated with these schools and with other techniques such as rolfing, co-counselling and rebirthing, will be aware that, in immensely short spans of time, profound and sensational patterns of experience are surfaced into consciousness and, to one degree or another, exorcised and re-resonated. We wish here to broadcast loud and clear the wonderful dispensation, the extraordinary opportunity that exists now in this form of healing for disciples and humanity generally.

The opportunity that exists now for healing is permanent and will be available for the rest of humanity's history upon this planet. However, we wish to accelerate the acceptance of the dynamism of growth that is inherent in these techniques. Indeed we feel that there should, in the metaphysical and New Age movement, be a celebration of the wonder of these techniques. We say this with due regard that these techniques can be misapplied, trivialised and worked with in a superficial manner, but with humanity this can happen to all good ideas and experiences. It need not, however, belittle the idea or the experience itself.

In saying that we wish to broadcast the exciting nature of these new techniques and encourage people to celebrate them, we are pointing out that here, perhaps more than anywhere else, you have positive proof that there are indeed profound changes taking place within the psyche of humanity and the planet in general. All across the Earth, people are experiencing subtle changes within the atmosphere and aura of the planet, experiencing the new resonances of the closeness of the mother/father cosmic Christ energies. Here, however, we are talking about something even more tangible: the visible, measurable and gaugeable growth and psychic changes that can be brought through astonishingly fast with these new transpersonal psychological techniques.

People will by now be generally familiar with the basic nature of these techniques which allow the individual to re-experience source events whose inherent resonance is so profound and dynamic that they continue to affect behaviour and attitude in the present. These source events can belong to the childhood of this particular lifetime, but the profound and important source events, which are the key to current patterns of behaviour, may go back historically many thousands of years. As the person in therapy re-experiences these events, they also — in a cathartic discharging manner — re-express them in a way that cleanses them of their influence upon the individual. This re-expression and cleansing of personal history is the major technique of the new psychological therapies. It is the technique used in the lengthy process of formal psychoanalysis through to the blisteringly fast depth therapy available in some transpersonal approaches.

There is a second set of techniques which works with memory patterns that are locked, not so much into the mental and emotional and psychological history of the individual, but into the etheric and physical memory patterns. These more 'physical' techniques, working with pure prana, release from the fabric of the physical and etheric body the memory patterns of traumatic events. The methodology of re-birthing for example, works primarily with the use of high-powered pranic overload and the patterns which are released are historical. To call it 're-birthing' is in a sense a misnomer, for what is in fact being rebirthed is the psyche of the individual at a physical-etheric level re-emerging from very old patterns of fear and anxiety locked into their physical cellular make-up.

The fact that these techniques and methods of therapy are available, is a clear demonstration of the exquisite and essential transition which is taking place on the planet at the moment. We would claim that we the Sparks are, in a sense, responsible for the efficacy of these techniques. We are not claiming responsibility, in terms of inspiration, for the actual method of the techniques. We are the electric love dynamism without which these techniques would not be effective.

This is not a boast — William is smiling wryly at the humour that he feels from us in this situation — but a statement of our purpose as an avataric energy coming into the planet. The great being who is the Avatar of Synthesis works at a macrocosmic level threading together the consciousnesses of all beings into the new modes of group consciousness. We work similarly in a microcosmic way. In healing we thread together the cellular make-up of the different aspects *within a single individual*. It is our synergetic effect in therapeutic situations that allows the cathartic discharge and release which brings about these immensely rapid changes. Our ability to do so is not so much a reflection of our inherent power to heal, but a reflection of the stage which humanity as a whole has reached in burning through its own past and preparing to launch itself into the future. Put another way, this ability for fast release and change is a reflection of the good karma that humanity has built up for itself. This is indeed a time of change.

Bless you and good night.

~~~~

Right, this is 28th August. Its 11.15 — continue the session.

We wish to make absolutely explicit the nature of the inner dynamics which makes the new forms of healing possible. It is indeed a grand claim that people can, in a half hour session of contemporary psychotherapy, work through historical patterns which in the past would have taken several years, perhaps even several lifetimes. This is indeed the case.

We wish to explain how the incarnation of the Avatar of Synthesis and the synergetic Sparks make this new development possible.

As we incarnate in the individual's psyche we create a new dynamic of multi-dimensional possibilities. This new dynamic is in the potential for new connectedness within the individual. We enhance the possibilities for various dimensions of connectedness, both within the psyche of the individual alone and within the connections with her environment — in natural, human and spiritual dimensions.

It is the nature of the consciousness of the Sparks to be expansively aware of each other continuously, simultaneously and in one and the same space. We say 'one and the same space' for although we may be located in different geographical spaces, in the way that you perceive space, we ourselves do not understand space in the same way and are interconnected in a consciousness transcending space. Space is for us a similar dimension to time. It is merely a form through which processes of expression of the Cosmic Mind take place. Our empathetic and telepathic rapport ignores space — or to be more exact, we ignore distance.

The moment that we incarnate into the psyche of a human being we create within that person the potential to interconnect multi-dimensionally with all other cellular life. The human being now holds the imminent potential for working with, in a flowing and fluid manner, the dimensions of past patterns, lives, histories and past fears.

Prior to our incarnation human beings existed, in consciousness, as if at the top of icebergs. In order to touch those levels of consciousness deep below, awareness had to pass down through strange waters. Awareness had to move into another dimension from the air in which it was normally located at the peak of the iceberg. From air to the waters of the depth. Our incarnation now creates an electric wave of subconscious awareness which expresses itself through the whole existence of your iceberg. We create within the surface of the human consciousness an ability to experience the gestalt which the human being is in totality.

At the same time, because of our expansive nature and natural ability to link out into the auras of the rest of humanity, we can create the possibility of a form of psycho-instrumental network that links you, the individual, with all the other beings who are connected with your history. When the individual is passing in healing and therapy through the catharsis of reliving the psychodrama of source events, our dynamic potential creates a psycho-instrumental networking with the individuals and gestalts who were involved in the original source event. We create empathetic, not karmic, links with those involved in the original situation that was the causation of a particular pattern within you.

We hope this is a new insight for you. In clearing

yourself of a pattern, you are empathetically facilitating the clearance of other people who were involved in creating that pattern in the first place.

It is shrewd and intelligent for people to become not simply aware of, but *experientially* intimate with the forms of therapy that are available — and to trust that the practitioners of them are sincere and compassionate.

We also want to explain the other distinct dimension of our work in healing.

The nature of our cellular networking creates an instantaneous flow of awareness between the ingrained memories existing in the physical, emotional, mental and conscious aspects of someone who is in the process of therapy, healing or transformation. Normally in human beings — especially people who are mentally focussed — there is little conscious contact with the fluid memory patterns that are lodged within the physical and emotional body. Children, on the other hand, have a natural ability to flow into an awareness of their physical and emotional states — and to integrate and to express them.

Many people who might be identified as mentally unstable or disturbed are also frequently playing with fluid ongoing awarenesses of their physical and emotional gestalts. However culture, education and their social environment give them no respectable terms of reference, no psychologically secure frameworks for expressing and playing with these awarenesses. Their mode of behaviour, therefore, detaches them from their culture, separates them from their human family and they move into ever-increasing idiosyncratic patterns.

The nature of the incarnation of the Sparks into the psyches of humanity is such as to evoke and recreate the playfulness which is a natural part of the creaturehood of the human being. People can begin to integrate themselves within the gestalt which is their total personality.

It is often considered that the personality is simply a construct of psychological attitudes. This is not the case. The total personality is not simply mental and attitudinal, it is also emotional and sentimental. By sentimental we mean empathetic, sympathetic and instinctive.

Each personality has its own distinct sets of sentiments. Individuals have different ways of relating to and responding to landscapes or sunsets. Some people prefer cats — they are cat people — and others prefer dogs.

Similarly, people have their own physical resonances in the way they relate to their planet — how they move through air, walk upon earth, or swim through water.

The experience now available to people is an awareness of themselves as a *total* creature. They are not simply individuals with psychological attitudes, making mental decisions that move them forward through time and space with their emotions and bodies following them.

We were going to end this part of the session here, but William has asked us to give you some exercises which would be pertinent to what we have been talking about.

First of all, we expect every well educated contemporary human being to be aware of the kind of exercises that are used in transpersonal psychology and the gestalt psychological movements. We were not going to give any exercises because of all the exercises currently available from these sources. However, we are intrigued to have been invited to actually create exercises in this *moment*. It challenges us to experience time in a 'fast' manner. We experience some amusement in becoming aware of time in terms of the seconds and minutes through which we must pass in order to become clear about the patterns we would wish to express to you.

The major point we want to make is that people should come into full self-conscious awareness of themselves as *physical* and *emotional* creatures without any feelings that the body or emotions need to be disciplined, or are in some way inferior to mental capabilities.

It is obvious that people require physical activity in order to be integrated, total personalities. As the saying goes, a healthy body is necessary for a healthy mind and vice versa. We are suggesting slightly more than that. We suggest that you should — no matter what your age or physical state — while sitting, moving or walking, take time every now and again to become fully aware of the miracle which is the physical machine that you are. This miraculous machine — your body, you — moves you through time and space. We are asking you, as you walk down the street, to be aware of the motion of your legs and the street passing beneath your feet as you push yourselves forward on the balls of your feet.

Become aware as you walk down the street of the air brushing against your face, of the temperature of the atmosphere against your skin. Be aware of these things. Be aware of the fact that your eyes are seeing, your ears are hearing, your nose is smelling, that you are even tasting the air around you. We are not asking you to do this for lengthy periods, just do this for a minute or so every day. It will bring you into contact with what you are as a physical human being.

You may also develop this awareness sitting down, as you become aware of your flesh pressed against the seat of the chair. Be aware of your body. More than that, be aware of the fact that your body is made up of many hundreds of thousands and millions of atoms and molecules, each one with a consciousness of its own, yet held together in the framework which is your consciousness. Be aware of this miracle.

As in your meditation you make yourself glow and expand into divine light, be aware of the cells and molecules and atoms of your body also expanding and moving into divine light. Be aware of the thrill which is the creaturehood of your physical body—not simply its totality and its ability to move, but also the cells and the organs which make it up*.

Become aware of the glory which is your emotional life, of the extraordinary depth of sentiment of which human beings are capable. Be aware of the extraordinarily inspiring affection which human beings are capable of expressing — the sense of bonding within a family or loved ones, the way pets are cuddled to you, the way you may embrace a tree. Be aware of the way in which music inspires you emotionally and sends currents of thrilling joy through the whole of your personality. Be aware of how, when rhythmic contemporary music is playing or drums are beating in rhythm, that your whole body responds in a certain sentimental and empathetic thrill to the resonance of the music. Be aware of your creativity that exists in your sentimentality and your emotions. Be aware of their purity and inspiration. Be aware of their essential nature within the totality of your personality. Be aware of all this and, with a sense of joy and detachment, you may find that by empowering yourself with this form of awareness, you may at the same time, defuse and disempower those emotions of negativity such as jealousy, envy and desire.

We do not feel that we need give you advice about the glories of the human mind. That is all too obvious. It is the predominating note of contemporary culture and completely out of balance. Be aware as a personality, of the way in which you are an *integrated* being. There is a tendency to separate the aspects of your personality and this is not appropriate. (It may be appropriate to do it in certain times of your life, but as a general theme this is

---

* We recommend that you read the 'Seth' books by Jane Roberts in this particular area.

not the case.) Your aspects play together and integrate. *You*, the real you who is incarnate in your vehicle, is incarnate through your emotions, mind and physicality. You are not separate — and in the same way that you are not a separate being — so your emotional, mental and physical beings are not separate but integrated in the total expression which is you.

We will talk in our next session about the role of the therapist, and our friends as counsellors and therapists, and people acting as therapists upon themselves.

Its twenty to midnight. End of session.

~~~~

This the 9th September. Its 11.20 at night. There's been a long gap because I've been away at Findhorn, but we did a couple of counselling sessions there. Okay.

There has been a long gap since the last session for the book and during this time we have done some counselling. This experience has had a strong impact on us as we move more fully into an experience of time, and the way human beings must pass through energy fields of internal friction as they transform themselves. This invokes in us that quality, unique to this planet, which we have come here to learn — compassion. In one of our counsellings we were jolted by a young person's poignant history and profound experience of loss and disorientation and his enormous spiritual aspiration. It touched us deeply.

However, we were about to enter into a discourse on the nature in which the therapist works inside the new forms of relationship. We have already laid out the basic method of healing available in contemporary psychology. You should also realise that the insights and wisdom of contemporary psychology have, since the War, married with the energies and potentialities of the Avatar of Synthesis.

The history of psychology in this century has to a degree parallelled the unfoldment of science. The early insights into the structure of the atom were, for example, reflected in the early insights of psychology concerning the nature of the hidden aspects of the psyche — the unconscious. As the structure of the atom, in terms of its electrons, neutrons and so on became explicit, so did the unconscious aspects of the human psyche. In both fields — science and psychology — what was hidden became obvious.

It was demonstrated, through psychoanalysis and Freudian theory, how these hidden unconscious aspects of the psyche influenced and governed apparently conscious behaviour and action. This was similar to the understanding of the atom. The discovery of the quantum theory showed that the movement of energies between particles *within* the atom is actually the dynamic major force in terms of the interaction of atoms. The *apparent* behaviour of atoms is not simply the behaviour of atoms-as-billiard balls, but is in fact the behaviour of internal forces manifesting externally.

Later, as a result of quantum theory, information began to be threaded together. It became clear that the atom and all matter were very dense forms of energy capable of extremely high-powered discharges — each atom containing nuclear power. This was parallelled in psychology by the theories which recognised that repressed memories, repressed psychic stuff, could in fact be released in a form of high-powered energetic discharge. This was recognised in early Freudian theory as the catharsis available in the re-living of experience, and later the Reichian theory in particular recognised the actual discharge of energy required for psychic relief — though we would suggest that Reich was inappropriate in his interpretation of 'orgone' energy.

The explosive force capable of being triggered in the atom, resulting in the horrific weaponry of the post-war years and in the nuclear power available to fuel electricity, is reflected in the extraordinary expansions of consciousness now taking place within the psyches of humanity. Nuclear explosions are parallelled by explosions of consciousness. Hidden forces are dynamically at work.

All this will become clear to you if you understand the parallelling — the working in the same gestalt — of the unfoldment of the nature of the atom with the unfoldment of the nature of the psyche. It is helpful to perceive this because it provides the framework in which our own incarnation of the Sparks becomes more easily understandable.

Therapists should be aware, as most are, that in working with human beings, they are dealing with *energy beings*. This energy being — you — is made up of pools, and seas, and reservoirs of energy beneath the apparent conscious personality patterns and beneath the apparent behaviour modes of the individual.

Equally, therapists need to be aware that, in order to effect change, there must be a discharge or release of energy in order for there to be a form of quantum leap within the psyche of the individual — here the parallel between sub-atomic physics and psychology is exact. We would like to point out here that in science, quantum leaps are made in minuscule distances and across electronic orbits; quantum leaps should be understood not as galactic new stretches of the imagination but as natural leaps in energy between one state of consciousness and another as part of an ongoing process.

The therapist works as a manipulator of energy-imagery and brings into consciousness certain source events from the past. These can be brought into the present and transformed by the new attitudes of the individual and discharged out into the general atmospheric pool. These techniques, however, have been limited by the tubular effect of time. The individual in therapy could work only — and this may seem perfectly ordinary and understandable to you — with the experiences that belonged solely to her or to him, could work only with the pools of psychic energy which were historically isolated and unique to that individual. The incarnation of the Sparks and the general repatterning created in psychic culture by the Avatar of Synthesis has now dramatically enhanced the potential of therapy.

The potential is enhanced at two levels. First of all, it is dynamically expanded at the level of the individual, as our incarnation intensifies the inter-relation between the different aspects of the individual psyche. We create a real empathetic gestalt between the vehicles — emotional, mental, physical and spiritual — as well as between all the cells. Everything in the body and the psyche is interconnected and mutually aware. The relationship between mental memories and where those memories are anchored into the cells of the *physical-etheric* body is now bridged into a single gestalt. This means that a release in one energy body, or one set of cells, immediately resonates through to other bodies, aspects and cells within the individual. The client, patient, human being — you — can much more easily create that quantum leap of internal energy which will create complete release into healing and transformation. Release in one aspect will then allow release in another aspect of yourself.

In the old forms of psychoanalysis the release was in many ways purely mental, with the emotional energy coming up through the safety valves of the mental vehicle, and being expressed in an elegant and safe manner. This was obviously the rhythm of three years of lying down on a couch three times a week. In the modern therapies, because of the new interrelation of the cellular vehicles of the psyche, physical, emotional and mental discharge can take place simultaneously, thereby creating personal releases of a fantastic kind not previously available.

The second expansion comes because the incarnation of the Sparks has for the first time introduced the fact that in some situations — though not all of them — the individual, in the process of transformative work, is in a gestalt interrelationship with the other consciousnesses, individuals and histories related to that person's specific state. What we are stressing here is that, as the individual works through a particular pattern towards healing and thereby transforms, discharges and reintegrates their energy, *they also release all other beings who are in one way or another interwoven with that particular pattern.*

There may for example be a past life pattern involving a small group of individuals who over a long period of time have chosen to incarnate as relations, parents, offspring, siblings, intimates, grandparents and so on. Over millennia, certain patterns of their individual karma are interwoven into a group karma. Now, in our present time, if one individual from that group goes into therapy — for example, a young woman whose pattern is a grievance against a particular parent — that young woman, as she releases herself through transformation and discharge of those original energies, releases not only herself but also creates a helpful wave of karmic release for the other people within that particular network of group karma.

If you as an individual clear yourself of a particular pattern, you are now also to a degree — though not completely — triggering and helping with the work of clearing that pattern within the whole group. Do not interpret this as meaning that the work that you do upon yourself is dissipated, dissolved or lost — though even if that were the case it would not be so bad in terms of service to the group. What we are saying is that through the gestalt interrelationships we have created over the last twenty-five years that, when you clear yourself, you are also clearing, in a dynamic fashion, for the rest of your group. This is not the same as simply alleviating mass karma. It is not the same as that pool of energy, that pool of circumstances, which is humanity's karma and with which every individual works. We mean something much more specific and incredibly dynamic in terms of release and relief.

What we are talking about here is the specific disentangling of severe psychological difficulties that exist in the most tedious, intense and convoluted way in human groups. We ask you to be aware of the fact that working through and becoming aware of patterns, and transforming them into clarity, releases not only you, but also those individuals who helped create the patterns with you. This may appear to be an ironic paradox for many of you, as you may feel that specific other individuals are directly responsible for having created the pattern in you in the first place and are responsible for your pain and difficulties in clearing the pattern. This may be the case, but you must understand the dynamics of the new energy situation are that you are clearing for them also. This transcends the petty but understandable resentments of your own psyche. You are living in a state of natural forgiveness and grace toward other members of your group whether you choose to or not. By clearing your pattern and therefore helping to clear the patterns of others, you are in a dynamic energetic way *forgiving* them with a force of psychic power that also releases them! You do not even have to try to be forgiving. What you do have to do is move with the greatest sincerity, purity, watchfulness and self-awareness that is possible in order to take yourself through and out of those patterns.

This all has clear ramifications for therapists. By 'therapists' we also mean friends counselling each other and individuals working as therapists upon themselves. Therapists, working within the new syndrome, must attune themselves to the general environment within which their clients exist. They must sensitise themselves to the particular incarnationally patterned relationships that their clients may have. For example, they should perceive their clients' parents, close friends and relationships not simply as coincidental members of a psychodrama but as intrinsic figures within a general pattern requiring therapy. At the same time, therapists can become more aware of the fact that the work that they do is evolutionary, sacred and more spiritually energetic than they have previously suspected. As a final comment on that, we would add that if therapy for their clients is part of a process of spiritual transformation, then surely that is what their own lives are about too. Therapists should apply the same criteria to themselves.

Okay. We're stopping at 11.46.

~~~~

Its the 13th September. The time is ten minutes to eleven. Its night-time in the flat.

We have enjoyed the counselling we have done over the last few days very much. There has not been a lot of it, but it has been challenging us to come into far greater resonance with the rhythms and attitudes of distress in human life. We find this educational and useful for our own evolution. It touches us deeply. We would like people who read this material to be fully aware of the way in which we, whilst having expanded extra-spatial consciousnesses, need to grow and enhance our own dimensions by becoming attuned to the human experience. We hope that you will feel some reassuring compassion and sympathy as you learn about our education. Within the emerging spiritual culture there is a tendency for humans to believe that the new dispensations bring about a psychic existence devoid of all pain, suffering and hurt. There are some who believe that people will, as if in one creationist moment, enter into a permanent and enduring sense of grace in which all hurt is melted. This is not the case.

The dispensations which we are talking about, the extraordinary giant leaps forward in consciousness, expansion and healing, will all take place within the framework of the general dynamics which have always existed in human incarnation.

The general structure of the game is still the same. You — Spirit, incarnate into the matter of the vehicle which you have created, your personality, and over time your resonances — you as a spirit and you as personality, will gradually come together as one. This process occurs through a mechanism of energy friction as your two vehicles meet and, through what some call 'alchemy,' brings the resonance of the personality into attunement and harmony with spirit. This process hurts. It is experienced as psychic friction — and psychic friction is experienced as moods, depression, pain, vulnerability, stress and all the *normal* symptoms of the human condition. We stress that this is the normal state for all human beings. The problem is not with that state — most of you handle it with a certain amount of gracefulness. The problem is that when you become more sensitive and aware of the spiritual psychic dimensions of your life, you tend to change your attitude towards the pain and *you take it too seriously*.

The problem is in your attitude to the pain and not in the nature of human existence.

If your attitude to your own state is one of amused detachment with a deep empathetic compassion for the natural way of your beingness, then you move gracefully forward through time.

The purpose of this particular session is to discuss the nature of drugs in relation to human consciousness. First of all, any drug is but a substance caught in three dimensions — atoms bound together in molecules in certain ways — each atom having its own consciousness and the molecules structured together having their own gestalt consciousness. When these small units of mineral consciousness are introduced into the human physical cellular network they have effects on some of the natural functions of the vehicle. The drugs we mean are those which affect the chemicals created by electric impulses within the human brain and which alter the general modes of consciousness of the human being.

Change in consciousness does indeed come about from a change in the biochemical make-up of the human brain. But this is not to say that consciousness emanates from the brain. The brain *anchors* consciousness and processes it into the physical vehicle. Consciousness exists 'out there' and, chemically affected, the brain can come into resonance with a consciousness not previously experienced. This applies to states of paranoid distress as much as to states of ecstasy.

There are two ways of appreciating the mode in which drugs affect the brain. The first mode is one which perceives the drug that is entering into the human system as being a dynamic form of mineral consciousness. We use this phrase, mineral consciousness, whether the drug is derived narcotically or from organic substances. We very much like the notion that the organic drugs such as marijuana, peyote, psilocybin and mescalin could be described as avatars of the plant kingdom. It can be perceived that, as the essence of the marijuana or the psychedelic enters the body, that a small consciousness — dynamic mineral or organic consciousness — is entering into the body with a powerful chemically programmed awareness of how it can play with the cellular structure of the human body as a whole. The programmed chemical consciousness of the drug has an awareness of the completed state into which it wishes to take the whole human organism. It does this by working partly through the way in which the brain accesses modes of consciousness and partly through the way in which the brain, as the regulator of the nervous system, can affect the sensations of the physical body.

The second way in which the substances work is directly upon the electrical discharges emitted by the brain. Electro-chemical stimuli in the brain trigger the production and excretion of particular hormonal substances. The hormonal substances, in turn, affect the frequency, the nature and the harmonics of the brain cells. What should be appreciated here is that a major function of brain cells, especially those upon the surface of the brain, is to act as receiving points or anchors for information that is more sensitive than simple touch, feel, taste, noise, smells and sights. The information here may be emotional or intellectual, intuitive or directly spiritual — but whatever the information is, the brain has still to *anchor* that information in order for the human being, in full consciousness, to register it. The drugs change aspects of the brain so that the brain can anchor down information usually inaccessible to it. The information exists 'out there' but the brain is usually not sensitive to it.

The point that we want to make concerns the therapeutic usefulness of some drugs and the fact that we ourselves have been able to utilise and work with the effects of some of these narcotics. We realise that these statements may cause some surprise, judgmentalism or even distress among some readers who would prefer to place all drugs into a pigeon-hole of being bad, unpleasant, unnecessary or destructive. However, we would point out that the way in which these small organic and mineral avatars enter and affect the body can bring about extremely fast movements through difficult psychological processes.

It should be recognised that in all times and cultures there have been respectable, acceptable, groups of people who used drugs recognising the sacramental nature of that usage. Recently much academic anthropological attention has focussed on the way certain hallucinogenic drugs are used to enhance the shamanistic paths of pre-literate peoples. Regardless of whether or not you are in resonance with, or appreciate this form of culture, you, dear readers, are not so prejudiced as to ignore the fact that the purpose of this drug usage was of a profound spiritual nature. The spiritual experience placed the taker of the drug in harmony with the essence of nature and the environment, and in resonant illumination of various forms of solar and cosmic energy. The taking of hallucinogens in these cultures was sacramental and part of the natural priesthood.

This brings us now to LSD, which was developed after the last War. This development parallelled the scientific advances that were taking place in relation to nuclear power. In mainstream science, the processes to unlock nuclear power were achieved. In chemistry, there was a similar move forward with the fabrication of this chemical. It should be clearly understood that the major mode in which LSD was originally taken was a sacramental one for contact with spiritual experience, inner self and transcendent states — despite the fact that the drug was developed for therapeutic purposes. LSD, in our opinion, had far too dynamic and powerful an effect in creating intense and extremely fast chemical changes in the brain which smashed the psyche through to gestalt cellular awareness in a way that was, for many people, harmful.

During the late sixties, however, the power and beneficent effects of the drug were experienced, because there were so many people taking it who were linked in an incarnational and subjective pattern of change which emerged as a mass movement across the world — flower power.

Now that the cultural energy field has changed, we ourselves do not recommend the use of LSD except in certain very carefully monitored circumstances.

William is tired and we shall continue this session tomorrow. That's fine. We close the session at ten past eleven.

~~~~

This is 14th September. Its 11.20. I'm at home in the flat.

We would like to present to you now certain ways in which narcotics can be, and already are being used for therapy.

During the late sixties and early seventies the psychedelic chemical LSD was being widely used. The nature of the experience was for many people not simply one of the high mystical experience frequently called 'white light,' but was also a profound sensation of belonging to a new family. This was a family whose members were the 'flower children' — and people who experienced themselves as flower children recognised each other. There was a period, when all over the western world as well as some parts of the totalitarian states, young people — and some older people — who had had the experience of psychedelic drugs could immediately recognise other people who had been through a similar experience. They now shared a new perspective on the world and recognised each other simply by eye contact. Many people were bemused by the fact that they could recognise their new family so simply — without words — and in the decades since there has been a sense of loss that the family did not continue.

What we would like to point out here is that this aspect of being a flower child which led to the experience of family was induced by the vibration of the Avatar of Synthesis and the Christ Sparks. The dynamic explosion of consciousness that they passed through by taking psychedelic drugs, met the startling new energies coming into the planetary system. Those people who had shared a startling expansion of consciousness during the same period due to the drugs, also subjectively — but not in their full brain consciousnesses — experienced themselves as cells within the same being. They were each a being within one single macrocosmic flower-child. When they walked the streets and recognised each other, they were telepathically and subjectively tuned into the fact that they were cells sharing the same gestalt. Most people who had that experience could not understand it. This is in a sense evidence of the incarnation of the Avatar of Synthesis and the Christ Sparks.

End of that session. 11.42.

7

The Actor in the Real World

All right. This is the 16th September. Its ten minutes to midnight. I should do these sessions earlier. I have no idea what today's session is about though I have an intuition that it may be towards the end of this book. We shall see.

*W*illiam *was wrong in thinking we are about to complete these sessions. We actually have a substantial amount more to do. This is the beginning of a new chapter which we would like to entitle 'The Actor in the Real World.'*

We are now concerned to offer some very practical applications of everything that we are trying to impart. This is also our attempt to make our own mode of incarnation into planetary life here clearer.

These are our ideas of how it might be possible to live more gracefully upon this planet in a way that is both conducive to your own happiness and to accelerating the general process of change for your species upon the planet, and all species that are related to you.

Risking criticism of repetition, we would like to state that the general picture we have been presenting to you, the reader, is one in which there is a new reality in terms of your relationships with your own inner selves, and with all the other selves which make up the various bodies which exist upon this planet. What has occurred in the last 25 years is that what was previously merely a mystical ideology — that you are all linked and as one — has now become reality. You have indeed always been linked and as one at a deep subjective, or what you call a 'soul' level, but this sensation of unity and at-oneness was not, in fact, a cellular reality.

Now how does this affect the way that you might choose to lead your life?

That is a huge and demanding question and we are aware that there are various patterns with pupils and gurus which we would wish to avoid. We would like you to pursue this discussion as fellow playmates within the same playpen. It is just that our mode of activity and inter-action is different from yours. But this difference is not based in our historical backgrounds. We could have been as you are now and you might have been as we are, were we to have commenced our journeys of cosmic service in different times and spaces. So do not read what we are saying with any form of profound seriousness. Listen and hear carefully what is it that we wish to say, but listen and hear carefully as you would give your attention to a close friend whom you honour and for whom you have a profound affection. Believe us when we say that we have a profound affection and honour for you.

We are in awe of and celebrate the deep sense of compassion and sensitivity that you are capable of expressing as a species — and this is indeed a profound lesson for us. What you can value about our attitude is our natural sense of cosmic consciousness and sense of the playfulness that exists through the whole of creation. It might seem that we are closer to the mystery and divin-ity of all life. However you human beings have your own proximity to the source in your deep ability to be com-passionate. It is the Divine Compassion which not only holds all creation in being, but also draws it into the future, and the fulfilment of its potential.

To use a more classically philosophical turn of phrase, we would ask you to consider our relationship with you as one that is dialectic. We would teach and communicate with you in a Socratic mode, but with a full awareness that you might be *our* Socrates just as much as we might be yours.

We ask, first of all, that you understand the information imparted in this book not simply as an ideology that stimulates your awareness and expands your consciousness to become more fully in tune with the true nature of the cosmos. We ask you to genuinely meditate upon the reality we are suggesting to you. You cannot do this, of course, if the ideas sound stupid and incoherent or glamorous and sensational. If, however, your intuition tell you that what we present here has some value, then we ask you to integrate it in a manner which is fully grounded. We are struck, as we experience and become more attuned to the lives of human beings, by how readily humans profess to believe something yet do not act upon that belief. We are astonished by the number of people within the new age movement who have an awareness of this or that, but it in no way affects their behaviour. We think particularly of healers who do not heal themselves and counsellors who do not counsel themselves, but see their roles purely in terms of an external environment in which they are an objectified actor. This, of course, is a nonsensical way of interacting with your own beliefs. We are aware of the danger of having a belief, but if you have a sense of the map and meaningfulness of inner life, then it is surely appropriate to act upon it.

Equally, if the information that is presented in this book rings a bell of illumination, then you must surely consider how it will affect the way you choose to live your life. We have already put forward certain distinct exercises which couples, for example, can do with each other. In particular, we would emphasise again the awareness two individuals in a relationship should have of being the major ecological environment within which they have responsibility — and that the couple should spend regular time attuning to this responsibility, attuning to what they give each other and what they, as a couple, give out to the world.

In the same way, we ask you as you pass through ordinary social life, to hold an awareness of the intimate and intricate pattern of relationship which you possess with every other single life form you encounter. This is not a philosophical platitude whose purpose is to lull you into a sense of mystical contentment with your environment. Our purpose is to underline and stress the profound and extraordinary relationship which you have with your environment and which your environment has with you. As you move through your social life, be aware that the level of interaction which is apparent to the five senses is but the tip of an iceberg of reality which is affecting, in an extreme and dynamic fashion, all of you. We ask you to be aware that the energy which you emanate as you walk into a crowd, the attitude which you put out, ripples in one form or another through the other individuals of that crowd. The energy that you put out does not simply evaporate.

How often do you walk into a situation and monitor what quality of energy you are putting out in that given moment? Energy follows thought, feeling, emotion and action. If it is your sincere desire that humanity pass into the future, accelerating the level of healing and cleansing of the planet, then it is crucial that each of you takes responsibility for your thoughts, feelings and actions. When we refer to actions we are not simply referring to physical actions. We mean the whole rhythm and oscillation of energy that goes into any physical action and then echoes out from it.

Imagine for a moment a room of people having a pleasant party. An individual enters that room and aggressively shakes hands with another. The handshake is complete and finished, and apparently the physical action is over. However, the energy that went into the handshake has not disappeared. That energy reverbarates and moves through the room as a reality in its own right. The quality of energy which was created in the handshake continues to exist — and will continue to do so into eternity unless it is absorbed or transformed. Thus it is that — and we hope that this amuses you — there is a kaleidoscopic cosmos consisting of nothing but handshakes!

Consider how many handshakes have taken place upon this planet since the beginning of humanity's existence. That energy continues to exists *right now.*

Now sense an embrace, a cuddle, a hug. What is the quality of the energy that goes into these embraces? That quality of energy — and the thought behind it and the expression of it — continues to exist. We know that those of you who have studied esoterics or subjective realities at all, are at least intellectually aware of the fact that 'energy follows thought' and that this energy floats around in clouds of a similar quality or atmosphere — in energy-forms which people can intuitively be aware of. People may also be influenced by them and . . . .

> *A bit of a pause while I went into meditation separately. It is quite interesting. When I lift my consciousness too high in meditation I lose the Sparks completely. Then I feel as if they are integrated as part of me — or their energy is — and they cannot communicate with me. I have to bring my consciousness down in order to allow them a kind of address into my mentality and brain-cells. Anyway . . .*

. . . . the point we are trying to make about the nature of action and the energy that goes with it must be clear by now. But do you act on that information? Do you go into situations aware of the quality of energy that you are putting out? If you accept the reality, and the subsequent responsibility, that the energy you put out not only continues to exist, but also has an intertwining effect on the environment, then it seems absolutely necessary that you look to the quality of the mood and attitude which you put into your actions. Can we ask that you put this awareness into every single sequence of actions into which you are entering? We are not going to demand it, though gurus in the past have slammed their staffs down on the ground and demanded that their students be permanently aware second by second of the reality of what they are. We are making no such authoritative demands. We are instead attempting to seductively evoke from you a natural and interested sense of responsibility for the real being that you are, and the effect that you have upon your environment. This will also add a beneficial dimension to your experience of reality.

For example, a disciple in a political situation may, at a personality level, consider themselves disempowered and unhonoured in that situation. This, however, is only one level of reality. There is another more effective and more dynamic level where she is dynamically affecting the situation for all other beings there. That individual, in a bad or good mood, creates and sends out the energy of that mood which influences the other people there. There may, or may not be, an observable effect or clear results. Who knows when an appropriate energy-attitude will have its effect? The results may years or decades or even centuries later. Be beautiful now.

Accept the lack of effect you have sometimes. You may be in a situation where you do not like the energy and attitude, but can't seem to affect it. That is absolutely fine. Your purpose is not to affect the situations that you are in — your purpose is to be aware of what you are putting out. For example, you may be in a situation surrounded by authoritarian figures sounding out a note you do not like. You feel disempowered and disadvantaged.

Be aware that the energy you are putting out is one of feeling disadvantaged and disempowered. You are also probably putting out some judgmental energy. It is not useful to judge outside of yourself. Be aware of what you are doing, what you are emanating. Your responsibility is the energy which *you and you alone* are putting out. That is your primary and major duty.

Any judgments which you are making of the situation around you are irrelevant and illusory. The attitude and energy which you are putting out when you are judging or reacting is an attitude of judgmentalism or reactivism. Is that what you wish to put out? Understanding the intimate nature of your ecological interdependence with all other life forms you must take responsibility for that which you put out. Do you believe this?

Its 12.26. End of that session.

~~~~

This is Thursday 17th September. It is 10.30 in the evening at the flat.

We wish to talk here about the nature of astrological effects upon humanity and about the other extra-spatial energies that affect the planet.

Readers of astrological columns in the daily press are coming in contact with a notion which hints at a profound phenomenon, no matter how shallow it may appear in its popular presentation. The underlying suggestion of the horoscope columns in the national media is that all people can be grouped according to their sun sign and, simply by sharing that sun sign, a common experience will be had during a particular period. Five hundred thousand Taureans will read that they will have good or bad luck with money or love on a particular day. This degree of shallow generalisation is precisely the reason why intelligent thinking people — or people who think they are intelligent and thinking — dismiss astrology.

Through the ages, mystics and esoteric astrologers have been fully aware that there are energies which come into the planet which do indeed affect the behaviour patterns, the atmosphere and the attitudes of people. They have recognised that astrological energies also have a general effect — and this has been carried on into this present age by some of the sophisticated astrological charts that are created for group entities such as the birth of a nation, the initiation of a particular group's work and so on. We are not here going to deal with the initiating forces of astrology nor with the structures and psychodynamics that set up a horoscope in the first place. Rather there are two points that we wish to discuss — firstly the fact that everything is interconnected and, therefore, when a particular astrological or ray energy is coming through, it does mean that people are being affected in similar ways.

Now, again, this is one of those pieces of intellectual awareness — that we are all affected simultaneously by astrological or ray energies — which is ideologically known but not experienced as a reality. The importance of experiencing it as a reality is that it allows one's egocentric self-centredness to be expanded to a perception of one's experience which includes all other people. An example would be that if a particular energy is coming through which creates tension, stress and depression, then knowing that this is also having a similar effect on other people — the mere acknowledgement of that reality — takes you out of yourself and creates a detachment from the experience. You are not going through the process on your own. It is not just you.

There are two lessons which we wish to offer here.

The first is one that we have just placed before you — that when energies are coming into the planet, they do indeed affect everyone and are not one person specific. In relation to this we would suggest that when individuals are depressed, or elated, or in any particular mood which is sufficiently strong to take them away from their centre, they should deliberately take time to sit in quiet and contemplate whether this extreme mood belongs solely to them and is part of their own incarnational growth pattern, or whether it is indeed an atmospheric energy pattern which is coming in on a planetary basis and affecting *everyone*. In merely moving into this awareness of others, you can detach yourself from the egocentricity of thinking you are the sole recipient of such an experience. You can then expand your consciousness to include and to empathise with others.

Two helpful things occur here, do they not? One is that the detachment allows you to centre and become aware of how you as an instrument can best play the music of the incoming energy so as to best process yourself through time. As you become aware of the effect the energy is having on other people, you take yourself into a state of empathy and sympathy which leads you into expressing, both mentally and emotionally, compassion — into *being love*.

We would like to place in italics the following point: *When you experience an unusually strong mood, stronger than your normal centredness, take time in silence to discover whether it is just yours or if it belongs to everyone.*

The second point that we wish to make is that the incarnation of the Avatar of Synthesis and of our own incarnation has meant that the inter-connectedness that occurs when there is a general incoming energy is far more dynamic and intense than ever before. We would like to give a practical example.

Suppose an energy is coming through whose pur-

pose is to create a point of tension which will allow people to experience their past with great intensity in order
to facilitate change. In experiencing their past, people will
feel very uncomfortable as they go through their patterns
of resistance to change. At the same time, imagine another
energy coming through which vibrates with the seventh
ray Aquarian resonance of fluid adaptability to all things
new. This 'new' energy can create an extremely tense psychic friction within people. So there are the two energies
coming in: the first intensifies personal history and awareness of source events, and the second forces one into open
surrender and fluidity.

This particular type of event actually occurs quite
frequently. They can come into manifestation at the time
of the new moon when one of the planets is squared or in
opposition to Pluto. The points we are making here again
is that first, everybody is experiencing a similar effect. The
second point is that, because of the cellular inter-connectedness of the individuals experiencing it, if one person becomes clear in the process and begins to move
through it with a certain amount of detached centredness,
then they will begin the release of energy which will free
all the other people within the cellular gestalt from the
patterning which creates the resistance.

What we are stressing here is the responsibility that
each disciple has to respond in a wise and intelligent way
to your own discomfort or ecstatic elation, when this is
the result of a general energy effect on humanity. You
should realise that, in having your experience, how you
react to it creates a resonating oscillation that passes out
through all other human beings within the network. In
the most general sense, this network is the whole of
humanity.

What we are asking for is conscious action. We are
asking you not to accept that this as another interesting
piece of mental information which you can store away in

your paradigm of holism and inter-connectedness. Can you afford, in terms of your self-respect, to continue with your surrender to moods? Is it not time to hold your centre — for yourself and everyone else?

Here is something which we know will encourage and interest you. The beatific beings, the saints, the liberated transcendent consciousnesses, those who have been human beings but are now pure spirit, also experience and respond to the energies. They too, who still choose to work within the planetary field, are part of the same network which is humanity. If you choose more consciously to link with them and respond to the incoming energies in a similar fashion to the way that they do, you will put yourself in tune with a new mode of processing these external energies.

At a more basic level, when you notice that you and others are experiencing a certain astrological energy which creates friction, you could, for example, look to Mother Theresa, Sai Baba or any being to whom you relate as having a beautiful consciousness. Examine how *they* relate to that kind of energy. As you relate to them, you will put yourself in resonance with a new way of responding to that energy. You will also, in a cellular sense, be open to a more noble way of responding to difficulties and strain. You can choose to do this exercise with any being whom you relate to as being beautiful.

You are not alone. We ask you to be aware of your responsibility to people who are less aware than you. We also suggest that you accept that there are other consciousnesses, far more aware than you, who are also responding to these energies. In a cellular sense, you work together with them to create a new cultural fabric.

As always, the underlying lesson here is, that it is helpful in all circumstances to take silent time and quiet space to reflect upon, come to a centre and be aware of what is really happening. In that silent space, choose, in the greatest clarity you can reach, how you wish to behave and what attitudes and energy you wish to radiate.

8

Between Groups and Groups

This is the 29th September, half-past midnight.

Thus far we have discussed the relationship of the individual to groups and to the greater group which is humanity. In this session we wish to deal with the relationships between groups themselves. We want here to point out first that groups tend to interact as anthropomorphic personalities. As energies come into the planet — ray energies and astrological energies — individuals in groups react in similar patterns. This patterned behaviour manifesting in a number of people, makes the group appear to have a personality distinct unto itself. For instance, on a very large scale, we have national groups in which incarnating souls have chosen to take on a particular culture of a specific, geographically defined area.

When a particular ray or astrological energy comes through, it affects all human beings upon the planet. However the way in which people are actually affected is coloured by the history, characteristics, astrological foundations and ray foundations of the group of which they are a part. Thus it is that when a certain extra-planetary energy comes through, the effect on the English people may be an attitude of indifferent passivity, while in another national group the same energy could evoke an attitude of sentimental nostalgia. Another energy may trigger an aggressive reaction in one group, while in another it may generate compassion.

In the same way that the resonance in a single cell of an individual can reverberate through all the cells of that human body, so the resonance in a single human being can reverberate through a group of human beings. Equally, a particular resonance in one group can reverberate out through all the other groups with which it is in contact. Thus, at a psychic and inner level, when a group of people who form a nation behave and resonate in a particular way, this has a reverberatory effect on all other nations.

When a group joins together for some form of political activity it puts out a certain resonance which has a reverberatory and harmonic effect upon all the other groups with which it has a relationship. That relationship can be tangible and physical, or subjective and telepathic.

It is possible to observe at an external and objective level the way in which political actions create direct effects, but at a more subtle level the energy of the group is also working in a way that affects all other groups. You will remember that in our earlier section about relationships and couples, we suggested that the two individuals within the relationship reflect upon not simply what they are putting into the relationship, but what the relationship itself is putting out into the local ecology and environment. Groups also put out a particular emanation and set of vibrations into the environment. It is possible of course, for a *small* group to sit, take time out and be reflective about the energy they put out to their local environment. You might imagine the workers in a shop sitting down on a weekly basis and discussing, not the turnover within the shop or the goods that have sold well or who the customers have been, but on a purely subjective level commenting on the atmosphere that they as a group have put into their local community. At a highly subjective level this shop group could perceive the energy of their group resonating up and down the high street in which they operate, affecting all the other groups which make up the community of that street.

At the same time, the group that is self-reflective can look at how its energy affects the general nature of the locality in which they work — or even how it energises the people who make up the group which is the Chamber of Commerce. If you believe it is far-fetched to think of a group in a shop being self-contemplative in this way, just remember the number of spiritual-holistic shops that exist, many of them spiritual centres for their locality.

It makes sense, for example, to imagine the staff at a school sitting down on a weekly basis, taking silence and contemplating carefully what they as a group and their school put out into their environment. This weekly activity could take place not simply amongst the staff, but also with the staff and students together. The students could contemplate what they emanate and how it affects that other group which is the staff — and vice versa. Equally there is the canteen staff who could identify themselves as a group, as well as maintenance and caretaking staff. All these groups could come together and examine what the school as a whole is resonating out into the local environment, the local community.

You should begin to see by now the self-awareness that could be brought into operation. We are painting a scenario of a very sophisticated and elegant culture, and what we are describing is not going to come into general manifestation for a long time yet.

It is possible for groups and communities who do accept spiritual and multi-dimensional realities, to take on board *now* this way of looking at things and to accept that they have certain responsibilities. We are suggesting that these groups monitor the clarity and effectiveness of their purpose, as well as the quality of their relationships, thereby acknowledging what they radiate to their environment.

Let us be absolutely clear that the dynamism of the energy which is resonated out into the atmosphere is extremely powerful. It is not simply that the group energy radiates outwards in a diffuse and general way, but that in reality it has a direct effect upon other groups. We would like you to contemplate the reality that, at a subjective and inner level, groups are all in dynamic inter-relationship. We exist within each other. If a group within a particular community emanates a hostile atmosphere two things occur. First, obviously, that bad atmosphere simply radiates outwards to be picked up or transmuted or transformed in one way or another. Second, other inter-related groups will, in a subjective way, be dynamically affected and react to it. That reaction, in the first place, will be subconscious, inner and subjective. The subconscious, inner reaction to the hostile atmosphere may be fear, defensiveness, intimidation or aggression. This inner reaction will, in some form, manifest in an explicit, outer reaction.

An example that can be drawn on is the aggression of the group that was Germany in the 1930s. At a subjective level this evoked certain reactions from other national groups. Some national groups were triggered into defensive-aggressive stances which indeed worked out into actual aggression. Other national groups, at a subjective and inner level, were intimidated and made fearful by the aggression of the German national group. This reaction of intimidation and fear manifested in the pacifism and neutrality, for example, of some of the Scandinavian states. It might have seemed that politicians were making clear political decisions — and at a certain level they were — but it must be recognised that politicians were also working within a powerful national atmosphere of subconscious reaction. Politicians could not make decisions without taking full account of the national 'mood' — the subconscious reaction — which is objectively definable as 'public opinion.' We are suggesting that the political decisions to be neutral in World War Two were, in fact, the decisions of politicians sensitive to the mass mood. This mood, of course, was the manifestation of the inner subconscious reality of being intimidated and fearful.

How a particular group responds to any set of energy circumstances depends upon its karma and history. To understand the behaviour of groups at a psychic level, one must attune oneself to their history and unique pasts.

This awareness is transferable to community life, specifically where there is a great deal of sharing of resources. Groups — informal and formal — that exist *within* communities must look to see what it is that they are radiating. The kind of groups that we are thinking of are work groups, and those who share similar spiritual ideologies or similar emotional attitudes. These groups may get together simply to do a piece of practical work or even just for fun. However, if they are clearly recognisable groups they should take responsibility for the fact that the individual members, acting together as a group, form a gestalt which radiates an energy which is greater and different from the energy of each of the individuals. These people should take time every now and again to contemplate and reflect what they are radiating to the rest of the community. Are they simply behaving in a manner that reinforces their own identities and does nothing for the general community? How are they interacting with other groups? There may be a small group of people who share a theatrical interest and come together for dramatic displays. Is their energy stimulating, reassuring and creative for other groups, or is it in fact nerve-wracking for other groups?

Be also aware that there are spiritual groups working in multi-dimensional inner planes, whose sole purpose is to emanate joy, love and creative peace to all other groups. This is worth meditating on.

It is also worth spending some time seeking, in a totally silent and quiet way, to identify these exquisite mystic inner groups whose glorious dynamism is a flame of continuous energy working to stimulate and regenerate all groups upon the planet.

End of that Session. Its one o'clock.

~~~~

Right, this is 19th September. Its Saturday. Its half past eight in the evening.

We are painting a picture of the dynamic interdependence and interpenetration of all life-forms that exist upon this planet. This also exists between life-forms throughout the cosmos.

We would also like to point out, that no matter how sophisticated the consciousness, no matter how much individual consciousnesses appear to be separate, they are always part of, and in relation with, groups. Moreover all consciousnesses, no matter how unique and separate they might appear to be, when they are in groups, radiate an atmosphere which is different from that which they radiate as single individuals.

The whole is greater than the parts — and the *quality* of the whole is different from that of the parts.

This can be for better or worse. Some groups emanate an atmosphere far worse than that which they could produce as individuals. Other groups radiate saintly beauty, transcending the limitations of the individuals. Our work is to encourage you to be aware of your group relationships and always, within the gestalt which is a group, to radiate more beauty and love than you do as separate units. Can you resist such an opportunity?

The purpose of this book is to seduce you the reader into an awareness of the subjective forms of consciousness of which you are an inalienable part. The individual reader may wish to reject all notions in this book, but this reader is nevertheless — like it or not — subjectively and esoterically a living part of group consciousness. No matter how much you pride yourself on your own individuality, you are also dancing and entwined and expanded in group consciousness.

You have patterns of relationship which connect you with various different groups simultaneously. Each individual has patterns of relationships which are historical and belong incarnationally to groups of friends and family with whom, as in a swarm, you tend to incarnate — and with whom you work out certain subjective and psychic patterns. We have already discussed how one person within a group, making an effective change or clearance, vibrates out that change to release other people from the same pattern.

Another form of group with which you are involved, whether or not you recognise it, is the group of people whose *souls* are similar to yours. This may be a new awareness for many readers. Souls resonate in a particular way depending upon the vibration with which they were first emitted from the Original Breath that brought all life into being. Souls form patterns with other souls of a similar resonance in the way that they change, serve, incarnate and then draw back into the path to Source. Each individual is a unique soul, but also shares certain characteristics and colours with other souls. As souls, moreover, you exist in a way that is similar to the Christ Sparks. As souls you are in complete attunement with each other, completely group-aware, because your consciousness as souls is in an energy field of at-oneness and pure love attunement.

Our job is to help you *as personalities* become aware of what you experience *as souls*. The awareness of mystic unity is, for you, a major proof of the reality of group consciousness. In mystic unity you know everything is interconnected and of one source. You could choose to know this more often, could you not?

Individuals are dynamically interconnected with other souls of a similar resonance — on a similar Ray*. When one individual within a particular soul ray group moves forward to be liberated from a certain pattern, that liberation echoes out through the whole soul group of which he or she is a part. We can call this soul group a true 'ashram.' This is an ashram, however, which is not externalised into physical reality but exists subjectively. It is an ashram within which and with whom you work in a telepathic manner and in which you join with your fellow members in your dream bodies.

Our purpose here is to dynamically stress the interdependence, the profound interpenetration that exists between fellow members who are in the same soul group, in the same ashram. You should, therefore, feel an increase in the weight of responsibility upon your shoulders when you recognise that the slowness with which you move spiritually forward creates an effect which can hold back others in your ashram. Equally, you should recognise that when you move forward *rapidly* into spirit, you accelerate the movement of everybody else in your ashram. Someone else's fast changes, in turn, help yours. You may also enjoy becoming aware of the fact that within each ashram there are extraordinary and exceptional beings of liberated consciousness whose sole focus and purpose is to help accelerate and draw you through your processes

---

*For a helpful analysis see Alice Bailey's books on the Seven Rays, particularly Esoteric Psychology Volumes I and II.

of clarification to a point of Freedom.

There are also other groups that you influence and which influence you, whether you wish to or not. These groups are the cultural patterns into which your incarnation has landed you as well as the cultural patterns within which you chose — whether you are conscious of the choice or not — to work.

Earlier we suggested that groups in work places take time together to become attuned to what they emanate into their environment. Parallel to this should go the awareness that you are a member of the cultural group within which you work. Equally, you are a member of the national group into which you were born. For example, if you emanate a particularly intense patriotic atmosphere-energy, this will influence and affect all other people within your national group. If at a subjective level you have an attitude of detachment from nationalism, then that pattern reverbates out to the group. You can take responsibility, to some degree, for the nationalistic fervour — or lack of it — in your culture.

See what your national group is radiating into the world community. It is important for individuals to recognise, particularly in the problem area of international politics, that they are parts of national groups. Their own, apparently private, subjective attitude towards their nationality has an effect on the total national attitude. Energy follows thought and, in your own private way, you can work within the great arena of international relations. We would like to see a loosening up of the attitudes of patriotic fervour and ideological attachment to the nation. We would like to see people who wish to invest loyalty and emotional attachment, to put that energy into humanity as a whole or into their specific local area. If you are going to be patriotic, why not be patriotic about the block of apartments or row of houses within which you live. Be responsible to the people around you. If at any point, however, you find that your sense of patriotism leads to any aggressive attitudes to outside groups, be very careful and self-aware.

It seems pertinent at this point to acknowledge that we have hardly used the word 'Love,' or 'Unconditional Love,' at all. This is because the total nature of our existence and resonance is one that is flowing musically, in merged empathy, with the energy and atmosphere and dynamic that is Love. In our teaching — in what we would like you to learn from us — the foundation for everything is Love. Your criterion for judging the appropriateness of all your thoughts and actions is surely Unconditional Love.

Take a pause. Our next section will be about animals, plants, minerals, cosmic beings and human beings.

9

Animals, Plants, Minerals, Cosmic Beings and Human Beings

This is the 28th September. Its 11.15 in the flat in London.

We want now to bring to your attention the patterns of relationship within the group consciousness of the planet as a whole — the relationships that exist between the different realms in nature. We specifically want to discuss the natural realms of the mineral, plant, animal, human, the super-human and the devic/angelic.

We wish, as always, to take what is a set of ideological ideas which are intellectually known and to represent them in such a way as to force your consciousnesses into accepting the interrelationships as an experiential reality. We wish to motivate you, not simply with the truth of the experience and the fact that you are living within it second by second, but also by reminding you once again that what we are discussing here is concerned with a highly intricate form of spiritual ecology. In a sense it would be possible to retitle this book, 'Spiritual Ecology'.

We have discussed in some detail the relationship and the energetic aura that is put out by two individuals in a coupling relationship, and that which exists within small and large groups. What we are concerned with here is the relationships which exist between the realms. There are several levels, several scales, from which this scenario can be surveyed. They range from a scale which is concerned with the total planet, through to the scale which is concerned simply with the individual.

Let us begin by observing the nature of the interrelationship of the total planet. It could be perceived, from an external perspective, that the major life-form that dominates the planet is the dense physical body, the mineral realm of the planet as a whole. This is interesting, because there are other planets and systems where there is hardly any dense materialised form. In fact there are planets and systems where the most dense form is etheric and therefore cannot be perceived by the human eye — though the energies of these planets and systems can be picked up as radio waves.

The body of your planet is made up of mineral consciousness interwoven with a form of devic life. You might recognise this devic existence at a frivolous level as being attuned to what is mythologised as gnome life. In other cultures the more profound aspects of this earth devic life have been mythologised as dragons or the great earth worms of tradition.

The gnomes at the surface of the earth, and the great earth worms and dragons beneath the surface, are representative of the undulating consciousness of the dense mineral planet. In the three-dimensional world, there is indeed the earth's crust which is several miles thick; beneath the crust there are areas of molten fiery mineral which erupt forth through volcanoes. What exists below that molten layer is a mystery to contemporary science, but we are prepared to suggest to you that that there are, towards the core of the earth, forms of mineral existence of a density and an electromagnetic resonance currently unrecognised by modern science.

The consciousness of this dense mineral body of the

planet responds to lengthy cycles of time and pressure. In a sense, *gravity* and time are the two dimensions which work to effect the major changes of consciousness in the mineral kingdom.

However, that there are many different forms of consciousness in the mineral realm. These manifest through all the various forms of the mineral realm: metals, rocks, crystals and so on.

Those consciousnesses of the mineral kingdom which are ready to move beyond that realm — for instance, radioactive crystals — incarnate into forms of life which, in the first instance, demonstrate their new mode of consciousness by transcending gravity and time. In three dimensional existence, plant life — the next manifestation of consciousness beyond the mineral realm — demonstrates the beginnings of an independence from gravity and time. A plant's primary movement is upwards and away from gravity. In terms of time, the plant realm's cycles of growth are immensely more speedy than those of mineral beings. Compare the cycle of a bush with that of a piece of coal.

In animals the relationship with time and space/gravity is again substantially altered. And in humans there exists the continuous potential for human consciousness to absolutely transcend time and space.

Seen from the outside, in the general flow of time and space, minerals, animals, plants and humans express different facets of one continuum. There is one single flow in space and time, with various consciousnesses and realms relating differently to the dimensions in which they seem to manifest. All life is the manifestation of a single breath of creation, a breath that is vibrant, active, interconnecting and embracing everything, you, plants, minerals, animals, all in one great and single awareness. You are all manifestations of the same wave.

Circulating through the plant kingdom, from the

tiniest sprout through to the most glorious redwood, are currents of wind, of air. These currents, these sylph consciousnesses, flow around, above and beneath the plants, the animals, and humans. Air is vaporous *mineral* life. You are surrounded by it.

Notice also the flow of water all around you — water is flowing mineral life. Look how much water there is in your body. You can understand here the *actual* interpenetration of the realms. In physical manifestation, there is no separation, only a dance, a continuum. In a very clear biological sense, the human is indeed animal. In a clear chemical sense, the human is indeed mineral. Look also at the food chains. These are all intimate inter-relationships.

The physical environment determines, in an ecological sense, the nature of the plant and animal life which can exist within it. And the relationships between all forms of life move in long-term cycles of symbiosis, which are of mutual benefit. In these cycles the general rhythms of growth, explosion, decay and decline are mutually helpful and necessary.

The human realm, however, provides, as a whole — and we are thinking here of the many millions of beings incarnated upon the planet — a dynamically new and different form of swirling psychic life which moves, dancing, tornadoing across the surface of the planet. The human being tornadoes himself in the dense physical planes of vehicles and furrows through the earth. These furrows make not only small channels where seeds can be sown, but also huge channels which are the conduits for highways and motorways. The human realm also interpenetrates with the earth realm in its removal of minerals from earth and in the banging, melting and electrifying of them into new shapes and forms of mineral life.

In its most extreme form we can see the relationship between humanity and mineral life exemplified in the conversion of mineral life into energy. This energy then flows into great factories and industries which are only of benefit to the human species.This is well noted in the current awareness of the ecological movement, particularly since the industrial revolution. At the same time that the dense physical relationship between the human and mineral realm is created there is, parallel to its obvious manifestation, an immensely dynamic inner and psychic relationship. For example, the mining of coal and then its use for the production of electricity, will in turn provide the power in a factory to makes cars. Human activity — as energy follows thought — has created a huge amount of psychic energy.

Picture for yourselves the earth and the realms of nature smothered by the mass psychic emanations of humanity. This paints a somewhat vulgar picture, but we would like you to catch a hint of the power of the mass psyche of humanity and the way in which it smothers and engulfs the planet.

This mass psyche of humanity is, of course, sensitive and responsive to the atmospheric energy changes that are triggered by the various astrological and ray impulses. These impulses trigger changes in all humanity, across the planet as a whole. Thus, there are the apparent coincidences of disaster, or of inspiration, that happen simultaneously all across the planet.

What should be recognised, is that these mass happenings directly involve all the realms. The psychic atmosphere created by human beings penetrates the winds and the dancing air of the planet, and penetrates the movement of the waters through the planet. Remember, again, that the human body is made up mainly of water.

As you walk upon the Earth, be aware that the mass psyche of humanity directly affects the air and the wind and the mineral kingdoms. Be aware of your psychic effect and the psychic effect of the whole of humanity as you touch and move mineral in cars, domestic appliances and the concrete and metal which make up modern buildings. As humanity walks on and lives within the mineral kingdom, your psychic atmosphere affects the mineral kingdom, manifesting through deep, resonant vibrations that flow and undulate out through the whole consciousness of the mineral kingdom which is planet Earth.

This impact on the mineral kingdom can result, in extreme situations, in mass mineral reactions in the form of tidal waves, earthquakes and volcanic activities. We will not say more on this particular subject. There are several books which are published concerned with this area and we would leave it to the individual to meditate upon the macroscopic relationships that exist between the psychic energy-atmospheres created by humanity and the other realms.

We would now like to bring the focus to a more individual level and to say that what is true for humanity as a whole, is also true for the individual. You, the individual, live in an extremely subtle and sensitive interrelationship with the realms around you. It is objectively clear how this relationship works out. You probably know about the effect your personal psychic atmosphere has, for example, on the health of your pets and on your plants. It also impacts on and creates the general atmosphere in your home and your workplace. It also affects the general atmosphere of your block of apartments, or your street or village and goes towards affecting the atmosphere of the whole planet. Be aware of what you create.

This is one of the most fundamental lessons of spiritual ecology — that you have to take responsibility for and be aware of your effect on the beauty and harmony of your surroundings. This requires a tangible, daily effort to be caring towards these realms. The vibrations which you express anchor into the mineral, animal and plant life which surrounds you. It is not only what you do in terms of actions but also what you radiate in terms of psychic atmosphere. Watch your moods. Are you responsible for psychic pollution? Recognise that the vibrations which you put out will attract to you similar vibrations. It is sensible to be careful.

Be kind to the environment which is your body. Be aware that you are a unit within the mass psyche of humanity and, as such, working towards melting, or building, upon the mass karma of humanity.

We ask you, in meditation, to look seriously at the living dynamic of the realms in which you live. Do not simply be aware of the plants as an enhancing factor in your environment or a vehicle for fairy life. Be aware of the throbbing cellular life that moves from the roots up through the stems into the leaves and flowers — and the aroma and magnetism of the plants which then inter-penetrates, in a form of radioactivity, the air that surrounds them. Be aware of the intrinsic life of the plant and how your vibration and attitude directly impinge upon and affect that plant — just as that plant directly impinges upon and affects you.

Also be aware of any animals that live with you or close by you. Do not simply be aware of them as personalities which amuse or give you some form of gratification, but be aware of the throbbing dynamic soul which manifests through them. Remember the consciousness that incarnates in them and realise that the whole of that psyche is sensitive to and responsive to you and your vibrations.

Know equally the dynamic life that exists in the very molecules and cells of the brickwork that surrounds you. Be aware of the beingness of the mineral form upon which you walk, work with and which surrounds you.

We are not asking you to develop a romantic awareness in which you drift through life. We are suggesting that, in an ordinary anchored way, you be aware of your environment.

Be also aware of these dimensions as you walk around. It is an attitude that you can adopt which will amuse you. Many people now name and directly communicate with objects around them — this is fine and a clear movement in the right direction. We do ask you in meditation, however, to be aware and to examine life with a curiosity which is part of your education. Be aware of the general trends and atmospheres that exist, with you, in your locality and on the whole planet. Remember the interpenetration, the interrelationship, between the realms. And, if you wish, you may in your meditation choose to radiate out into these various relationships harmony, love, affection and friendship and a general sense of happy spiritual cooperation.

End of session.

~~~~

Right. Its the 7th October. Its 11 p.m. Quite a long delay since the last session.

We are very happy to be dictating again after such a pause. In the last section we dealt specifically with the relationships between the kingdoms upon the planet. In this section we want to draw your attention to the galactic and cosmic relationships which exist. Although these are to some extent expressed in contemporary astrology, people tend to miss that astrology is, in fact, the science of the relationships between cosmic energies. Astrology is not simply a mode of describing how a human personality is structured at any time. Astrology is the science and art of understanding the nature of the relationships which exist between the energy beings who are the whole cosmos.

Contemporary science, with its intellectual strictures, finds it difficult to accept astrology, but it should be appreciated that from a sub-atomic physicist's perspective all matter is energy. The energy body that is the Earth is a huge, dynamic, radiating energy being. It is not simply the physical body of the earth — or the electromagnetic, electric, physical body of the Earth — the earth energy body includes all the dynamic energies that belong to the mineral, plant, animal and human realms. Some of this energy is visible in the forms of dense matter, but there is also all the energy of the inner dynamics that are incarnate in all forms of life. The souls incarnated upon the planet create a whole energy realm in etheric, spiritual, intuitive, mental and emotional matter — all extraordinarily dynamic and radiant. The planet Earth is a throbbing being of extraordinary energy.

Macroscopically, of course, the system which we have just described as the planet Earth is but one part in a total system. Its centre is the Sun which has its own wonderful sets of energies and, orbiting around the Sun, the planets which, together with it, form this total Solar System. The Solar System is, at its level of energy, fantastically more dynamic and radiant and throbbing than planet Earth and its realms. The total solar system, seen from another star, a light year away, is a being not 'twinkling' — twinkle, twinkle, little star — but a cosmic entity *radiating* intense, dynamic forms of electric consciousness. This consciousness which emanates from the essential beingness of the Solar System — of which our planet is a part, of which we are a part — interrelates with, communicates with, dialogues with, all the other stellar star beings.

When people on this planet talk about communicating with Star Beings they are often interpreting the way in which they experience the energy which belongs to other stellar entities. These stellar energies, however, are not little star people several feet tall and dressed in aluminium. These stellar beings are star systems similar to the solar system and expressing a certain kind of energy which is the gestalt of that particular system.

Whether evoked or invoked, there is a harmonious resonance between other star systems and our solar system. The most famous star in relationship with our Solar System is the star Sirius. Sirius has been described in several esoteric traditions as having a relationship to our Sun, similar to the relationship in a human being between the soul and the personality. Sirius represents Soul. Our solar system represents Personality.

The Stars are in intimate communication with each other. They, in a very real form, speak to each other. When the ancients gave the planets and constellations names and anthropomorphised them into human form, they were not simply representing them in ways that made them more understandable to human beings; they were indeed describing them in a way which is accurate. The planets communicate with each other, just as the stars do. Stars, of course, form clusters and groups which themselves form particular gestalts. The astrological constellations are an example of this. In interpreting and understanding them, the constellations are given particular forms — animal, human and mythical forms. These beings communicate.

Earlier in the book we described the way groups of all kinds should be aware of the fact that they create a synergy of energy which, as a gestalt, they radiate outwards. We suggested that groups be self-reflective about this. What we are talking about now is the vast consciousnesses and personalities that make up planets, star systems, cosmic systems. At their own level of consciousness, they must also be aware of the energy which they emanate as a system or a group, and which they feed into the total system of which they are part. At that level of consciousness there is an intimate understanding of the energetic atmosphere and energies being expressed outwards into the cosmos. This intimacy is electric, we were going to say 'second by second' but this does not express what we mean because a sense of time is transcended by a continuous flow of consciousness that is absolutely *aware*. The consciousness of a Star is absolutely sensitive to that which it is emanating.

You can now begin to understand how it happens that the consciousness of the Solar System is aware of the happenings upon one of the planets in its system — the Earth. The Sun is aware of the energies and consciousness of each realm upon planet Earth. Our Solar System's consciousness is totally attuned to the energy put into it by humanity.

Humanity, as it moves forward in its particular purpose through time and space, reaches points of crisis and need. It is as if humanity, as an energy being, forms a vacuum of need which requires filling. The consciousness of the star system, the mind of the Solar Logos, is totally and completely aware of this need. This need is then sounded out from the consciousness of our star system, from our Solar Logos. Our star system — our Sun — is in direct communication with other stars, other solar systems, other galactic systems, who form with our system yet another gestalt. They have responsibility for the total gestalt.

These other star systems are in resonance with our solar system. They understand and experience, through continuous communication, through a non-stop *intimate* electric relationship, the needs within our solar system. We are talking, in this instance, about the specific needs of humanity. Humanity, in its passage through time and space, is required to go through a difficult change. It creates a vacuum of need and expectation in its own synergetic aura and this is recognised by the solar system. The solar system expresses this need outwards and it is, in turn, recognised by stars in communication with it. One or another star holds, within its own being, an energy which is appropriate to respond to the need of humanity. This energy then comes in response to the need and incarnates through the star or star system, through the Sun and then into the aura of the Earth and finally into humanity.

We are talking here about inter-stellar avatars, a form of energy and consciousness coming from another part of space into our solar and planetary system to answer a specific need. Indeed, we began this book by describing that we ourselves accompany the Avatar of Synthesis, who is just such a response in consciousness from another star system to a need within humanity. Humanity cannot progress through its next stages in time and space unless this need is answered. This need is for group consciousness. And this need will be answered by an energy-consciousness avatar that will help to create a synthesis in telepathic communication between all the cells that make up humanity. We ourselves, the Christ Sparks, are part of another energy within a stellar system, that accompanied the Avatar of Synthesis to facilitate this process.

And on that note we wish to conclude the writing.

By and large, we feel that we have made our point. Whether our point has been made successfully or not will depend on whether it helps the readers of this book to act in a way that is more aware in all the many different situations which you inhabit — to become more aware of the synergetic atmosphere you create with your various groups.

*Be aware that You **Radiate**.*

Further Work with William

If you are interested in cassettes or workshops by William, please write to:

Alternative Workshops
St James's Church
97 Piccadilly
London W1V 0LL

Introducing Findhorn Press

Findhorn Press is the publishing business of the Findhorn Community which has grown around the Findhorn Foundation, co-founded in 1962 by Peter and Eileen Caddy and Dorothy Maclean. The first books originated from the early interest in Eileen's guidance over 20 years ago and Findhorn Press now publishes not only Eileen Caddy's books of guidance and inspirational material, but many other books, and it has also forged links with a number of like-minded authors and organisations.

For further information about the Findhorn Community and how to participate in its programmes please write to:
The Accommodation Secretary
Findhorn Foundation
Cluny Hill College, Forres IV36 0RD, Scotland
tel. +44 (0)1309-673655 fax +44 (0)1309 673113
e-mail reception@findhorn.org

For a complete catalogue, or for more information about Findhorn Press products,
please contact :

Findhorn Press
The Park, Findhorn, Forres IV36 0TZ , Scotland
tel. +44 (0)1309-690582 fax +44 (0)1309-690036
e-mail thierry@findhorn.org

Other books by William Bloom published by
Findhorn Press

FIRST STEPS (£4.95) isbn 0 905249 85 2
An Introduction to Spiritual Practice

A helpful and friendly introduction to spiritual practice that
makes sense whatever cultural, intellectual and religious
background the reader comes from. It can be adapted by each
individual to suit their lifestyle and needs. *First Steps* sounds
a much needed note of unifying clarity in a time when there
are so many new and alternative approaches to personal and
spiritual transformation.

SACRED TIMES (£5.95) isbn 0 905249 76 3
A New Approach to Festivals

Birth - Marriage - Death - New Moons - Full Moons -
Equinoxes - Fire Festivals

William Bloom provides complete rituals for the celebration
of birth, marriage and death, as a basis from which readers
can create what is authentic for themselves. He also suggests
a comprehensive structure for a new age religion in which
the natural rhythms of the earth — the lunar cycle, solstices,
equinoxes and seasons — signal the major spiritual festivals,
and gives a detailed description of how to work meditatively
with the lunar cycle for spiritual service and personal transformation.

Books about the Findhorn Community...

THE KINGDOM WITHIN (£8.95)   isbn 0 905249 99 2
A Guide to the Spiritual Work of the Findhorn Community
Compiled and edited by Alex Walker

This collection of writings about the history, work, beliefs
and practices of the Findhorn Foundation and its associated
community of spiritual seekers offers a vision of hope, inspiration and encouragement. With contributions by David
Spangler, William Bloom, Dorothy Maclean, Peter and Eileen
Caddy amongst others, this book covers topics which include
nature and ecology, the art of living in community, the relationship of 'new age' thought to formal religion, and co-operation with the spiritual worlds. The world is hungry for the
hope and inspiration this book brings — and so are you!

THE FINDHORN GARDEN (£9.95)   isbn 0 905249 63 1
**Pioneering a New Vision of Humanity and Nature in
Cooperation**
by The Findhorn Community

The story of the early days of the Findhorn Community and
its communications with the nature kingdoms. Peter and
Eileen Caddy's experiences as co-founders of the community,
Dorothy Maclean's contact with the devas, R. Ogilvie Crom-
bie's (ROC's) meetings with Pan and the Elemental Kingdom,
and the wisdom of David Spangler and other combine to give
a unique perspective on the relationship between humans
and nature.

THE FINDHORN COMMUNITY (£8.95)   isbn 0 905249 77 1
by Carol Riddell

The author traces the community's development over the
years and gives a clear picture of the community today and
the new businesses and independent projects springing up
around it. The second half of the book includes a number of
intimate and revealing interviews with members, both young
and old, who share their lives and experiences of living in
this incredible community.

FOUNDATIONS OF A SPIRITUAL COMMUNITY (£5.95)
by Eileen Caddy   isbn 0 905249 78 X

Guidance that helped a family living in a tiny caravan
develop into an international spiritual community. The cen-
tral principle of turning within to find the true source of faith,
inspiration and love makes this book relevant not only for
those building a spiritual community but also for all who live
ordinary lives in our wider society.

THE SPIRIT OF FINDHORN (£5.95)
by Eileen Caddy   isbn 0 905249 97 6

This book offers a brief history of how Eileen gave up everything to follow her inner voice as well as sharing much of the
guidance and wisdom which supported Eileen through the
early days of her spiritual transformation and the birth of the
Findhorn Community.

Mail order information

In the UK, free postage & packing
In Europe, add £1 per book
Rest of the world, add £2 per book

Payment: by cheque made out to Findhorn Press, or
by Visa or Mastercard (please give number and expiry date)

Please send/phone/fax/e-mail your order to
Findhorn Press Mail Order
The Park, Findhorn, Forres IV36 0TZ , Scotland
tel. +44 (0)1309-690582 fax +44 (0)1309-690036
e-mail thierry@findhorn.org